The Bounce Back Workbook

The Bounce Back Workbook

Lynnette Khalfani-Cox

WILEY

Published by John Wiley & Sons, Inc., Hoboken, New Jersey.
Published simultaneously in Canada.

For general information on our other products and services or for technical support, please contact our Customer Care Department within the United States at (800) 762-2974, outside the United States at (317) 572-3993 or fax (317) 572-4002.

Wiley also publishes its books in a variety of electronic formats. Some content that appears in print may not be available in electronic formats. For more information about Wiley products, visit our web site at www.wiley.com.

Library of Congress Cataloging-in-Publication Data is available:

ISBN 9781394205196 (Paperback)
ISBN 9781394205202 (ePub)
ISBN 9781394205219 (ePDF)

Cover Design: Paul McCarthy
Cover Image: Getty Images: © Maria Toutoudaki

SKY10060316_112323

To all the people who have experienced stressful setbacks,
I admire you. You're still standing!

Contents

About the Author

Lynnette Khalfani-Cox, The Money Coach®, is a personal finance expert, speaker, and author of numerous money-management books, including the *New York Times* bestseller *Zero Debt: The Ultimate Guide to Financial Freedom*. Lynnette has been seen on more than 1,000 TV segments nationwide, including television appearances on *Oprah*, *Dr. Phil*, *The Steve Harvey Show*, *Good Morning America*, *The TODAY Show*, and many more. A former financial news journalist, Lynnette now co-owns TheMoneyCoach.net LLC, a financial education company that she runs with her husband, Earl Cox. Together, they offer financial education consulting services, courses, and workshops.

As a subject-matter expert on many personal finance topics—including credit and debt, saving and budgeting, paying for college, homeownership, and entrepreneurship and wealth building—Lynnette helps organizations of all kinds develop and roll out high-quality financial literacy programs and campaigns. She also creates financial education curricula and provides strategic counsel to companies, nonprofits, government agencies, or educational institutions that want to launch financial content, products, services, apps, or other tools. For her financial literacy work, Lynnette was honored with the Muriel F. Siebert Lifetime Achievement Award by the New Jersey Coalition for Financial Education.

Before starting TheMoneyCoach.net in 2003, Lynnette was a *Wall Street Journal* reporter for CNBC, where she covered business and personal finance news. Lynnette spent nearly 10 years at Dow Jones & Co. Inc. working as a reporter, bureau chief, deputy managing editor, and personal finance editor. Prior to her work at Dow Jones, Lynnette was a correspondent for *The Philadelphia Inquirer*, a writer, and an assistant producer for WTXF (FOX-TV) in Philadelphia, and a writer for the Associated Press in Los Angeles.

Lynnette earned her bachelor of arts degree in English from the University of California, Irvine. She also holds a master of arts degree in broadcast journalism from the University of Southern California as well as a certificate in FinTech (financial technology) from Cornell University. Lynnette is a native of Los Angeles who spent 20 years on the East Coast but now lives in the greater Houston area with her husband.

Other books Lynnette has written include:

- *Bounce Back: The Ultimate Guide to Financial Resilience*
- *Perfect Credit: 7 Steps to a Great Credit Rating*
- *Your First Home: The Smart Way to Get It and Keep It*
- *Investing Success: How to Conquer 30 Costly Mistakes & Multiply Your Wealth*
- *The Money Coach's Guide to Your First Million*
- *Zero Debt: The Ultimate Guide to Financial Freedom*
- *Zero Debt for College Grads: From Student Loans to Financial Freedom*
- *The Identity Theft Recovery Guide*
- *College Secrets: How to Save Money, Cut College Costs, and Graduate Debt Free*
- *College Secrets for Teens: Money Saving Ideas for the Pre-College Years*
- *Free Pre-College Programs*
- *Millionaire Kids Club Book 1: Garage Sale Riches*
- *Millionaire Kids Club Book 2: Putting the 'Do' in Donate*
- *Millionaire Kids Club Book 3: Home Sweet Home*
- *Millionaire Kids Club Book 4: Penny Power*

Introduction

Welcome to *The Bounce Back Workbook*, the interactive companion guide to *Bounce Back: The Ultimate Guide to Financial Resilience*. This powerful *Workbook* is designed to help you handle life's setbacks, learn from adversity, and become more financially and emotionally resilient in the process.

If you're like me, you've encountered your share of struggles. I call our 10 biggest difficulties "The Dreaded Ds"—and they include: downsizing from a job, divorce, death of a loved one, disability, disease, natural disasters, debt, damaged credit, dollar deficits, and discrimination.

As a money coach, and someone who has overcome 9 of the 10 Dreaded Ds, I know the pain and frustrations you may be experiencing. I also understand that these setbacks can have a profound impact on your life, emotionally, mentally, physically, and financially. So I'm here to walk alongside you as your guide and ally, providing the support and expertise you need to bounce back stronger than ever.

Activities to Engage, Inspire, and Empower You

Within these pages, you will find a wealth of practical exercises, strategies, and tools carefully crafted to guide you on your journey toward financial and emotional well-being. In *The Bounce Back Workbook*, we'll tackle each of your obstacles head-on, providing you with a comprehensive range of features and activities designed to engage, inspire, and empower you as you rebuild your life and your finances.

Here are the *Workbook* elements you can expect:

Reflection questions: Explore thought-provoking questions that encourage you to think deeply about your experiences, emotions, attitudes, beliefs, and behaviors regarding any Dreaded Ds you've faced. These reflection exercises provide valuable insights and self-awareness, helping you identify areas for personal growth and transformation.

Writing prompts: Engage in writing prompts that promote self-analysis, creativity, and exploration. These prompts allow you to express your thoughts, feelings, aspirations, and actions without judgment, fostering deeper understanding and personal development.

Worksheets: Utilize fill-in-the-blank worksheets and templates to capture your thoughts, goals, and financial information. These worksheets serve as valuable tools for tracking your progress, making informed decisions, and staying organized throughout your financial journey.

Goal-setting trackers: Set realistic and achievable financial goals related to each setback. The *Workbook* includes exercises that guide you through the process of defining your goals, breaking them down into smaller milestones, and creating action plans to achieve them. By setting clear objectives, you can work toward a future of financial stability and success.

Action plans: Based on your unique goals and needs, you'll develop step-by-step action plans for each of the Dreaded Ds. You'll also break down the strategies and advice from the main book into actionable steps for your specific situation. These plans will guide you in overcoming challenges and creating a road map to financial resilience.

Quizzes and tests: Evaluate your current financial situation and knowledge with brief quizzes and mini-tests. Don't worry! These aren't graded assessments. Rather, these tools will simply help you gauge your understanding of the concepts presented in the main book, track your growing knowledge, and identify areas for improvement.

Checklists: Stay organized and keep tabs on your progress with helpful checklists provided throughout the *Workbook*. These visual representations of your achievements will provide a sense of accomplishment and motivation as you make strides toward financial resilience.

Inspirational case studies: Gain inspiration and motivation from real-life case studies and examples of individuals who have conquered the Dreaded Ds. These stories highlight the resilience and success of others, providing you with practical insights and relatable examples to apply to your own circumstances.

Personal storytelling: There is enormous power in telling your own story. You get to describe events from your perspective and point of view. You'll connect with others. You'll deepen personal relationships. You'll have epiphanies. You may rid yourself of shame or unhealthy emotions. And you'll often realize you're not alone. Therefore, this *Workbook* also includes opportunities for you to tell your own story and write—or rewrite—your personal narrative.

Wellness exercises: Recognizing the importance of emotional and physical well-being, *The Bounce Back Workbook* includes exercises focused on emotional resilience and self-care. From journaling prompts to mindfulness exercises to stress management techniques, these activities will help you recover emotionally and physically, ensuring holistic well-being.

Collectively, these 10 exercises foster a deeper understanding of yourself and your relationship with money, better enabling you to make positive changes and develop healthy personal and financial habits. By engaging in these workbook elements, you'll gain the knowledge, skills, and confidence needed to overcome obstacles, develop resilience, and create a solid financial future.

But *The Bounce Back Workbook* goes beyond a mere collection of exercises—it is a personalized road map tailored to your unique circumstances. As you engage in various activities throughout the *Workbook*, these interactive elements will enable you to transform the general concepts outlined in the main book into custom-built prescriptions for your own life. This customization and personalization ensure that you can more intimately address all relevant topics and make meaningful progress in the areas that matter most to you.

Throughout this transformative journey, remember that you aren't on a solo endeavor. Although each one of us is unique, millions of other people have personally experienced the challenges you're now facing. As you draw upon the wisdom of those who have overcome these setbacks, and experts too, you'll reclaim your power and rewrite your financial story.

A One-of-a-kind Financial Toolkit

If you don't yet have *Bounce Back*, I urge you to pick up a copy to understand the main concepts and strategies I describe for becoming financially and emotionally resilient. Each section of the *Workbook* corresponds with the chapters in the main book, allowing you to deepen your understanding and employ the recommendations in your own life. Together, *Bounce Back* and *The Bounce Back Workbook* provide a one-of-a-kind financial toolkit to support you in overcoming life's challenges, fostering resilience, and achieving holistic well-being.

As you hold this *Workbook* in your hands, consider the possibilities it holds. Picture yourself engaging in powerful reflections that illuminate your path forward. Envision taking quizzes and assessments that unveil your strengths and areas for growth. Visualize crafting personalized action plans that empower you to prevail against the troubles you face. See yourself delving into real-life case studies, finding inspiration in the stories of others who have conquered adversity. And through it all, trust in the transformative power of your own journey.

Use *The Bounce Back Workbook* as your personal financial diary, to document your feelings about money matters, as well as your resilience, growth, insights, and progress. When you look back at what you've written—one month, or even one year from now—you'll see that this guide is also a testament to your determination and unwavering spirit. It is an invitation to embark on a transformative quest, guided by the wisdom, expertise, and support offered within these pages. Finally, it is an assurance that you need not figure everything out, all by yourself—I am here with you, every step of the way, as your companion and ally.

Get ready to bounce back stronger than ever and soar to new heights. Your future awaits.

The Bounce Back Workbook

Chapter 1

Resilience and Grit

In the main *Bounce Back* book, we explored the concept of the Dreaded Ds and how they can be viewed as transitions in our lives. In this chapter of *The Bounce Back Workbook*, we'll start by diving deeper into the three stages of transition: the ending, neutral zone, and new beginnings, as proposed by change expert William Bridges. These stages provide a framework for understanding and navigating the emotional, psychological, and personal aspects of change.

Remember: change is something *external*, which happens *to* you, and it's often abrupt. Transition is something *internal*, which happens *within* you, and it typically takes months or sometimes years. You may not have a say-so in whether or not something changes in your life—such as getting laid off or enduring the death of a relative. But you absolutely can shape your own transition, and how you process that change. One way to do that is to reframe your thinking. As awful as it is to get downsized from a job or to lose a loved one, for example, it's also true that life's toughest changes provide opportunities for positive transformation.

Reflection Activity: A Major Change in My Life

Instructions: Take time to reflect on a major change in your life and the resulting transition you faced. The change could be one of the 10 Dreaded Ds, or something else—such as retirement, marriage, finishing college, the birth of a child, or a big move to a new location. Consider the ending stage, neutral zone, and new beginnings stage as described in the Bridges Model. Write down your thoughts and feelings about each stage and how you navigated through them.

The specific change I experienced was: _____.

The change was (fill in the blank with "expected" or "unexpected"):

_____.

When this change happened, I initially felt: _____.

Today, when I think of this change, I feel: _____.

When this change happened, other people told me:

_____.

This change meant the end of: _____.

To deal with this change, I have done the following:

_____.

At this point, I would describe my transition as:

_____.

If I had to describe the level of stress I've experienced, I would say:

_____.

Most changes in life—even when good things happen—present some level of stress. How has the stress of the change you described above affected you overall? Describe your reality below.

Here's how the change I experienced affected me physically, emotionally, personally, and financially: _____

_____

_____.

All stress is bad for you: true or false? (Circle one and explain your answer below)

_____.

Are there any benefits to stress? If so, list at least one benefit.

_____.

Benefit #1: _____.

Benefit #2: _____.

Benefit #3: _____.

(**Hint:** In *Bounce Back*, I cited information from Sudden Money Institute founder Susan Bradley, who offered three ways that stress helps you.)

Personal Storytelling: Sharing My Truth

How comfortable would you be sharing your own personal story of a significant change or transition you experienced? If you are able and have a trusted confidante, describe the ending, neutral zone, and new beginnings stages and how they impacted your life. Reflect on the lessons you learned and the growth you experienced during this process. If you don't have anyone you can tell, simply record yourself talking about your experiences.

In this exercise, you can also share a personal story of a significant change or transition you have experienced where you have made it to the other side. Describe the ending stage, where you recognized the need to let go; the neutral zone stage, where you explored new possibilities; and the new beginnings stage, where you embraced a different future. Share how this transition has shaped you, what insights you gained, and how it contributed to your personal growth.

Goal Setting for Future Changes or Transitions

In *Bounce Back*, I explained that Certified Financial Transitionists are financial experts who help people get through various life transitions. These experts are certified by the Sudden Money Institute, whose founder added another stage to Bridges's theory of transition: a planning stage. A planning stage is helpful because "sometimes we get the ability to know beforehand that something is ending," says Stephanie Genkin, a CFP and Certified Financial Transitionist. She adds: "Many of us are in a state of financial transition and anticipation. We're anticipating events that we know are going to occur, like retirement, selling a business, or the death of an ill family member."

Identify one change or transition you are currently facing or anticipate in the near future.

What would help you get through this experience? What kind of support do you need to feel better? Additionally, if you knew that the change was inevitable, and there was nothing you could do to stop it, what goals would you have for each stage of the transition process? Write your answers to these questions below. As you establish goals, consider the skills, support, and resources you will need along the way. Feel free to also add actionable steps you can take to move through each stage and create a new beginning that aligns with your values and aspirations.

_____

_____

_____.

Writing Prompt: I Did That! Exploring My Own Resilience and Grit

Instructions: Resilience and grit play vital roles in navigating transitions and bouncing back from challenges. But sometimes we may not realize the existing strengths we possess or how we have successfully recovered from past setbacks. So reflect on your own resilience and grit by answering a series of self-reflection questions below. Explore how you have demonstrated resilience in the face of adversity and how grit has fueled your determination to overcome past obstacles. Identify areas where you can further develop resilience or cultivate a resilient mindset.

What does resilience mean to you, particularly financial resilience? How would you personally define financial resilience?

_____

_____

_____.

Reflect on your own level of financial resilience. Do you consider yourself financially resilient? Why or why not?

_____

_____

_____.

In what ways have you demonstrated financial resilience in the face of unexpected financial challenges or setbacks? Can you recall specific instances where you were able to bounce back from financial hardships? If so, how did you do it?

_____

_____

_____.

Consider the concepts of resilience and grit as discussed in *Bounce Back* based on work by experts such as psychologist Angela Duckworth. How do you see these traits playing a role in your pursuit of financial resilience? How can resilience and grit help you overcome obstacles and maintain balance in your financial life?

_____

_____

_____.

Reflect on the definition of financial health provided by the Financial Health Network. These are based on how well you save, spend, borrow, and plan. How many of the eight indicators of financial health align with your current circumstances? Which areas do you excel in, and which areas could benefit from improvement? Put an X mark next to each one as appropriate.

	Needs Improvement	Doing Great
Saving indicator 1: you have sufficient liquid savings		
Saving indicator 2: you have adequate long-term savings		
Spending indicator 3: you spend less than you earn		
Spending indicator 4: you pay all bills on time		
Borrowing indicator 5: you have manageable debt		
Borrowing indicator 6: you have a prime credit score (670+)		
Planning indicator 7: you have appropriate insurance		
Planning indicator 8: you plan ahead financially		

Also, consider the categories of financial vulnerability and financial resilience as defined by the Financial Resilience Institute. The four categories they describe are:

- Extremely vulnerable;
- Financially vulnerable;
- Approaching resilience; and
- Financially resilient.

You're *extremely vulnerable* if you simply cannot handle *any* outside shock to your budget or emergency at all. Such an event would cripple you financially or push you into a major crisis.

You're *financially vulnerable* if you'd be challenged by a *major* financial stressor, but you're living paycheck to paycheck, or are just getting by under normal circumstances.

You're *approaching resilience* if you're doing fairly well, and can even save and plan somewhat for the future, provided nothing *major* unexpectedly pops up or derails your budget.

You're *financially resilient* if you can easily absorb pretty much *any* financial shock or emergency, and it wouldn't affect you at all. You still can budget normally, save, plan for the future, and maintain good credit—even in the face of common yet unexpected events.

Where do you believe you currently fall within these categories? List some specific steps you can take to move toward greater financial resilience.

_____

_____

_____

_____.

Think about the relationship between different forms of resilience, such as social, emotional, physical, and financial resilience. How might developing resilience in one area positively impact your ability to become more financially resilient? _____

_____

_____

_____.

Remember the idea that resilience can be cultivated and improved over time. What steps can you take to enhance your financial resilience? What specific skills or habits would you like to develop to strengthen your ability to bounce back from financial challenges? _____

_____

_____

_____.

Consider the importance of planning and preparation in building financial resilience. How well do you currently plan ahead financially and have appropriate insurance? What are the adjustments or improvements you can make in this area? _____

_____

_____.

Take a moment to envision your ideal level of financial resilience. What would it look like for you to readily spring back from unexpected financial hardships? What obstacles do you face and what steps can you take today to move closer to that vision? _____

_____

_____.

Improving Your Financial Resilience and Grit

What does resilience mean to you? How about grit? Do you see these two qualities as being different, or do they go hand in hand? Let's delve into your level of financial resilience.

Instructions: Consider a hypothetical scenario where you are hit with an unexpected bill of $1,000. How would you handle it? Would it cause significant stress, or would you be able to manage it comfortably? Use this scenario to reflect on your current level of financial resilience.

If I got hit with an out-of-the-blue $1,000 bill, I would handle it by:

_____

_____.

From an emotional standpoint, a $1,000 emergency would make me feel:

_____

_____.

Instructions: Based on your self-evaluation from the previous exercise, identify three steps you could take to improve your financial resilience. Try to be as specific as possible. Simply identify and think about what you can realistically do, given your circumstances. No action is too small.

Action steps to improve my financial resilience:

Step 1: _____;

Step 2: _____;

Step 3: _____.

Getting started: to put the action steps above into practice, I will immediately do this:

_____

_____.

Case Study Analysis: Learning from Athletes and Others

Recall how I shared in *Bounce Back* that I'm a huge sports fan. I recounted numerous stories of athletes that have persevered and overcome enormous obstacles—such as pro surfer Bethany Hamilton, who lost her arm to a shark yet went on to be a surf champion, or NFL great Peyton Manning, who was written off after injuries yet proceeded to win a Super Bowl ring at age 37.

You don't have to be a star athlete to have overcome difficulties or what looked like impossible situations. However, there are insights to be drawn from circumstances where defeat seemed likely, but the end result was victory and a positive outcome.

What three words would you use to describe these athletes?

_____.

What lessons can you learn from their attitudes?

_____.

What takeaways can you glean from their behaviors?

_____.

Describe a past situation that seemed hopeless or as if it wouldn't work out, but it turned out fine:

_____.

What similarities do you see between your situation and these athletes?

_____.

What differences do you notice between your circumstances and theirs?

_____.

Instructions: Let's go deeper. To make the concept of resilience even more relatable, think of a time when you faced a significant challenge, setback, or hardship. Write down how you handled the situation, how you felt, what you learned, and how you eventually overcame (or are working to overcome) the adversity.

_____

_____

_____

_____

Your Resilience Role Models

You probably don't know those specific athletes. But you likely do have someone in your life who showed great resilience. Write about their experience and what you learned from it.

The point of this exercise is to identify and gain insights from resilience role models, whether they are public figures such as the athletes mentioned earlier or people in your personal circle.

Instructions: List three people you consider to be resilience role models. For each person, note specific behaviors, attitudes, or strategies they use to cope with adversity that inspire you.

Name of person #1: _____.

Inspirational qualities: _____.

What I admire most about how they've handled adversity is: _____

_____.

Name of person #2: _____.

Inspirational qualities: _____.

What I admire most about how they've handled adversity is: _____

_____.

Name of person #3: _____.

Inspirational qualities: _____.

What I admire most about how they've handled adversity is: _____

_____.

One way that I'm just like this person is:

_____

_____

_____.

One thing I'd like to do that they do is:

_____

_____

_____.

Moving from Judgment to Self-compassion

Hopefully, you were able to see some positive traits in the individuals you listed and think about how you might be able to emulate some of the characteristics about them that you find admirable or inspirational. But the purpose of the exercise above wasn't to compare yourself to that person or to other people in general. It's merely to highlight traits and actions that help people bounce back from adversity—traits anyone might aspire to in order to better handle life's setbacks.

Even with that knowledge, however, it can be hard to avoid being harsh or critical of ourselves when things don't go right, or when we fall short of other people's expectations or of the standards we set for ourselves. Under such circumstances, Saundra Davis, a financial coach and head of Sage Financial, says it's important to have compassion for ourselves, or something that she calls "unconditional positive regard."

"That means, my love for myself is not contingent upon my performance," she explains. "I care for myself as much—if not more so—when I don't live up to expectations, as when I do."

The lesson: when you're struggling emotionally with something, or even if you feel that you have failed in some way, it's healthy to strive to have "an attitude of caring for your suffering, acknowledging that suffering, and holding it with kindness," Davis says.

To foster kindness and self-compassion, and to recognize your current strengths, complete the two following activities: writing a self-compassion letter and acknowledging your existing strengths.

Activity 1: Self-compassion Letter Exercise

Now that you've read about the concept of a self-compassion letter in *Bounce Back*, it's time for you to write your own. Refer to the guidelines provided in the main book, and remember to focus on addressing your feelings and struggles, offering support, understanding, and encouragement.

Follow the steps and write your letter below.

Friendly Salutation: _____.

Acknowledge your feelings and struggles: _____
_____.

Express understanding and empathy: _____
_____.

Offer support and encouragement: _____.

Share practical advice or coping strategies: _____
_____.

Close the letter with kindness and affirmation: _____
_____.

Read this letter aloud to yourself and keep it in a place where you can easily revisit it when you need a boost of self-compassion and emotional support.

Activity 2: Recognizing and Embracing Your Strengths

Reflect on your life and the different challenges you've overcome. Consider the strengths that have helped you get through these hardships. Are you a good problem solver? Do you have strong communication skills? Are you adaptable? Are you persistent or creative? Has turning to prayer or family worked? Write down at least three strengths, or three solutions you've used, and an instance when each helped you overcome a difficult situation.

Strength 1: _____ Situation: _____.

Strength 2: _____ Situation: _____

Strength 3: _____ Situation: _____.

Solution 1: _____ Situation: _____.

Solution 2: _____ Situation: _____.

Solution 3: _____ Situation: _____.

Build Your Support Network

It's a privilege for me to be with you on your journey to financial and emotional recovery after you've faced one of the 10 Dreaded Ds. But you also need other people in your corner. Building a strong support network is crucial to fostering social resilience. In the following exercise, you'll identify the individuals you can lean on during challenging times.

Instructions: Make a list of at least three trusted people in your life who can provide support during times of stress or difficulty. Write their names and the reason why you chose them.

Person 1: _____ Reason: _____.

Person 2: _____ Reason: _____.

Person 3: _____ Reason: _____.

Write down a time and date (no more than a week away) when you will reach out to each person. During this conversation, be honest about your experiences, feelings, and any specific support you may need—even if it's just a willing ear to listen.

Person 1: _____ Time & Date: _____.

Person 2: _____ Time & Date: _____.

Person 3: _____ Time & Date: _____.

Remember, reaching out is not a sign of weakness. In fact, asking for support is a strength and a key part of building resilience.

After you have the needed conversations with the people listed above, come back to this chapter and jot down some notes about your discussions. For example, how did each person make you feel? What surprised you about the conversation? What did you learn during your talk?

Person 1: _____

_____.

Person 2: _____

_____.

Person 3: _____

_____.

Further Reflections

Think about the activities you've done or will do. What insights did you gain from the self-compassion letter? How do you feel about reaching out to your support network? Jot down any thoughts, feelings, or insights that arose while doing these exercises.

_____

_____.

Practicing Mindfulness and Self-care

It's important to also consider your physical well-being in order to build your overall resilience. Let's start by engaging in a mindfulness practice of your choice. But before we get into an exercise, it's important to understand exactly what "mindfulness" means—and what it requires of you.

Davis, the financial coach, is also a mindfulness coach. She notes that mindfulness really just means "focused attention." It's about noticing what is, including the environment, as well as your thoughts and emotions, without judging them. It's also about noticing what is affirming, positive, or calming for you. For example, I walk three to five miles each day with my husband, Earl. During our walks, I notice the things outdoors that are calming for me, such as the wind on my face, the lush green trees, and the serenity of the lake near my home. That's mindfulness.

In decades past, many Christians (myself included) shied away from talk of "mindfulness." For me, it seemed a bit woo-woo and out-there, if you know what I mean. Ha! I chuckle now at how my thinking (thankfully!) has evolved. And I'm far from alone. "Christians now accept mindfulness too," Davis notes.

So let's choose a mindfulness exercise. You can do one or both of the following:

(1) mindfulness breathing or (2) mindfulness in your daily life.

Option 1: Mindfulness Breathing or an Alternative Exercise

Performing a simple breathing exercise can help you reduce stress and increase mindfulness. As you go through this exercise, remember the instructions from *Bounce Back*: inhale slowly through your nose for a count of four, hold your breath for a count of four, and exhale slowly through your mouth for a count of four. Do this for 30 seconds to a minute, or longer if you'd like.

Afterward, reflect on the experience: How did your body feel during and after the exercise? What thoughts came to your mind? Did you feel any different afterward?

Write down your thoughts here_____

_____.

Mindfulness When You Have Physical Anxiety or Trauma

During our interview, Davis told me that breath exercises "aren't safe for everyone." She didn't mean that some people's lungs simply can't handle holding their breath for a few seconds. Rather, she explained, "For someone who has PTSD, some type of trauma, or who doesn't feel safe in their body, they may not feel safe with embodied practices." An embodied practice, or embodiment practice, is where you use the body as a tool to develop awareness, stay present, or feel whole. However, if—due to past trauma or other circumstances—you feel like your body is not safe, or not under your control, then breath exercises and embodiment practices may be triggering or make you uncomfortable. If this sounds like you, here are two alternatives that Davis recommends.

First, try simply engaging in active listening, where you intentionally listen for and notice various sounds that are nearby you first and then sounds that are farther and farther away. For instance, if you're in your living room or dining room, you might notice the hum of the refrigerator in your home. Then you might take note of the sounds of a neighbor or their kids outside. Then you may conclude by trying to hear the sounds that are as furthest from you as possible—perhaps a car in the distance or an airplane overhead. All of this requires focused attention and listening, which is a form of mindfulness and being present in the moment.

Another alternative is to take notice of something that's tactile: you can feel the fabric you're wearing or even touch the words on this page. How does your shirt feel? Is it soft against your skin or abrasive, tight, or itchy anywhere? As far as this book, scan your fingers along the words on the page. Feel the sensation on the tips of your fingers. If you're reading an e-book version of this *Workbook*, feel the Kindle or other reading device you're using. Does it feel like metal or plastic, or something else? Are your hands sweaty or tired at all from holding your e-reader?

Option 2: Incorporate Mindfulness into a Daily Activity

Instead of trying to create time for mindfulness and come up with an activity that involves focused attention, it may be much easier to just include mindfulness in some aspect of your normal routine.

"Most people can't start a mindfulness practice, or they view themselves as bad meditators," says Davis. And that's because it's often difficult to set aside time for a specific mindfulness activity—and then get your mind to cooperate on demand. Perhaps you seem to go off into never-never land and not be able to focus. If that's you, don't worry. You're not alone. This is very common. Davis's suggestion: Bring mindfulness into a daily activity that you're already doing. Then simply become more focused and attentive to the task at hand. You may cook dinner each night, for instance. Notice the sights and sounds of each ingredient as you touch, chop, or cook your meal. What colors do you see? How varied is your nutrition and what you're consuming? Don't judge yourself or criticize yourself if, for example, you don't have anything green on your plate. Simply take note of what is. Again, this is mindfulness.

Whether you set aside time for a specific mindfulness exercise or incorporate it into some daily activity, observe any resistance or attachments you may have toward change and practice cultivating a sense of openness, curiosity, and acceptance toward transitions in your life.

Develop a Self-care Routine

Developing a daily self-care routine can also significantly contribute to your physical resilience. Try to incorporate physical activity, relaxation techniques, and proper sleep into your routine.

Instructions: Write down what your ideal, daily self-care routine would look like:

Morning: _____.

Afternoon: _____.

Evening: _____.

Late night before bed: _____.

Commit to following this routine for at least one week. Note any changes in your physical or emotional state as you stick to the routine.

Writing Prompt: Visualizing Your Comeback

I love a good comeback story—and again, I don't think I'm alone in reveling in hearing about amazing stories of triumph. Isn't it inspiring to learn about people who overcome seemingly unbeatable odds and rise above those circumstances in a way few could have imagined? Some of us love to hear about rags to riches stories; that's one version of a comeback story. But bouncing back can look different for different people. So I want you to explore how you'd define a comeback—*your* comeback.

Remember the story I told you in *Bounce Back* about former Denver Broncos quarterback John Elway and the legendary victory he engineered known as "The Drive?" I want you to now visualize your own comeback story. Write a paragraph or two describing a future scenario where you successfully bounce back from adversity. What does your victory look like?

How do you feel? Who's there to cheer you on? Be sure to include the low points in your story and what helped turn things around. Don't hold back. Write something ambitious and inspiring!

Your comeback story: _____

_____

_____

_____

_____

_____

_____

As we conclude this first chapter of *The Bounce Back Workbook*, which focused on resilience and grit, take time to think about what you have just done, felt, and discovered. What emotions surfaced for you during the exercises? What lessons have you learned so far, and what growth have you experienced? Write a recap below.

_____

_____

_____

_____

Developing resilience is a process. It takes time, practice, and patience. Celebrate the small victories along the way. They're signs of your growing resilience and your ability to bounce back from adversity. As you complete these exercises, also remember that the journey is just as important as the destination.

Chapter 2

Building Your Resilience

Resilience is like a muscle: you can build and strengthen it over time with proper usage. In this chapter, we'll get you stronger by making you more emotionally, physically, socially, and financially resilient. We'll do this by delving into the essential qualities and strategies that enable you to cultivate resilience in the face of life's challenges. By developing a resilient mindset and embracing the power of emotional, mental, and physical well-being, you can navigate the Dreaded Ds with strength and determination.

And remember: resilience is more than just bouncing back. It's about possessing a state of mind that allows you to adapt, grow, and even *thrive* in the face of adversity. It involves practices that enhance self-awareness, emotional regulation, and a sense of purpose. So get ready to explore 10 core strategies that can help you strengthen your resilience, ultimately leading to improved financial decision-making and a more fulfilling life.

Let's begin with a quick recap of these 10 powerful strategies, as shared in *Bounce Back*. Whenever you're faced with one of life's tough battles, consider these strategies as the go-to weapons in your resilience arsenal that you can deploy as needed.

1. **Practicing mindfulness:** Mindfulness is a transformative practice that allows you to cultivate presence, reduce stress, and develop greater self-awareness. Through guided mindfulness exercises, you will learn to harness the power of the present moment and build emotional resilience.
2. **Cultivating gratitude:** Gratitude has the remarkable ability to shift your focus from the negative to the positive, fostering resilience and well-being. Through reflective exercises, you will explore the practice of gratitude and learn how to integrate it into your daily life.

3. **Journaling:** Reflective writing can be a powerful tool for processing emotions, gaining perspective, and identifying patterns of thoughts and behaviors. Through journaling prompts and writing exercises, you will uncover insights, explore your inner world, and promote resilience.

4. **Being patient with yourself:** Developing resilience is a journey that requires time and effort. It's essential to acknowledge that setbacks are normal, and progress may not always be linear. Through self-reflection and self-compassion exercises, you will learn to be patient with yourself and embrace the process of growth—even when things don't progress as quickly as you'd like.

5. **Practicing self-compassion:** This is an important aspect of resilience because none of us is perfect. Realize that there will be times you feel that you've messed up—or perhaps that the mess you're in is hopeless. It's at these moments when you most need a heavy dose of self-compassion.

6. **Seeking professional help:** Sometimes, we need support from professionals to navigate challenging situations. So you will explore the benefits of seeking guidance from therapists, counselors, financial experts, or other professional advisors who can provide valuable insights, accountability, or added support to help you reach your goals.

7. **Staying connected:** Building a support network of people who provide encouragement, empathy, and practical assistance is vital in times of adversity. Through activities focused on fostering connections and nurturing relationships, you will cultivate a resilient support system.

8. **Focusing on self-care:** Prioritize your physical, mental, and emotional well-being through self-care activities. Engage in activities that bring you joy, relaxation, and a sense of purpose. Regular self-care boosts your resilience and overall well-being. Remember to take care of your physical health, engage in hobbies, and set boundaries to maintain a healthy balance in your life.

9. **Establishing a new money game plan:** Recovering from financial setbacks requires a proactive approach to managing your finances. Establishing a new money game plan helps you regain control and build a stronger financial future.

10. **Creating a financial plan B:** Evaluating a variety of potential what-if scenarios and Dreaded Ds that could affect your finances will give you clarity about how you'd tackle each scenario. You'll also gain additional economic security and control over your future.

As you work through this chapter and focus on incorporating these 10 strategies into your life, I invite you to do three things: (1) Be open to self-discovery; (2) strive to embrace the practices shared, even if they don't initially resonate with you; and (3) trust in your inner ability to build resil-ience. In doing so, you'll boost your capacity to overcome challenges, seize opportunities, and determine your own best path forward no matter what challenges you face. Let's now put these strategies into practice, applying them and their related concepts to your life.

Practicing Mindfulness

As explained in the previous chapter, mindfulness involves being present in the moment, focusing on your thoughts, emotions, and physical sensations without judgment. By practicing mindfulness, you can develop a nonjudg-mental awareness of your inner experiences, cultivate emotional resilience, and navigate difficult situations effectively. Here are two types of activities and exercises to incorporate mindfulness into your life:

Grounding Techniques

Engage in grounding exercises such as body scanning or the 5-4-3-2-1 tech-nique. Body scanning involves paying attention to each part of your body sequentially. For instance, you might start with your feet, noticing how planted they are on the floor. Then you'd take note of your ankles and calves, moving up to become aware of how your knees feel. Are they comfortable? Or do you need a stretch? Next, notice your thighs, abdomen, and chest areas. Is your breathing slower or faster than normal, or about the same? Now move your attention to your fingers, hands, and arms, before finishing with your neck, face, and head. This process of scanning your body, part by part, brings a heightened sense of awareness and mindfulness.

The 5-4-3-2-1 technique involves identifying things you can see, touch, hear, smell, and taste in your surroundings. A better way for me to explain the 5-4-3-2-1 grounding technique is to have you do it. Take a moment to identify and write out the following:

Five things you can see: _____

_____.

Four things you can touch: _____

_____.

Three things you can hear: _____

_____.

Two things you can smell: _____

_____.

One thing you can taste: _____

_____.

How do you feel after this exercise? Write down your thoughts here:

_____.

Mindful Daily Activities

As previously stated, you can also incorporate mindfulness into your everyday tasks. Pay attention to the sensations, sounds, and details of activities such as eating, walking, or washing the dishes. This helps you stay grounded in the present moment and cultivate a sense of appreciation for simple pleasures.

Writing Prompt: Cultivating Gratitude

Gratitude shifts your focus from what's going wrong to what's going right in your life. It fosters resilience, well-being, and a balanced perspective during challenging times. Try the following exercises to cultivate gratitude:

Gratitude Meditation

Find a quiet space where you won't be disturbed. Close your eyes and bring to mind something or someone you're grateful for. Spend a few moments focusing on the feeling of gratitude. When you're ready, write down your experience here:

_____

_____

_____.

Daily Gratitude Journal

Keep a gratitude journal and write down at least three things you're grateful for each day. This practice helps you intentionally focus on the positive aspects of your life, developing a habit of gratitude. Begin now by simply listing three things you appreciate.

One thing I'm grateful for is: _____.

A second thing I'm grateful for is: _____.

A third thing I have gratitude for is: _____.

Since you may not yet have a journal, you can also begin a daily gratitude practice within this *Workbook* to jump-start your efforts. Write down three things you're grateful for each day for one full week.

Day 1: _____.

Day 2: _____.

Day 3: _____.

Day 4: _____.

Day 5: _____.

Day 6: _____.

Day 7: _____.

Reflect on the week: Did you notice a change in your perspective or mood as you focused on gratitude? Write what you noticed:

_____

_____.

Expressing Appreciation

Share your gratitude with others by expressing appreciation for their actions, presence, or support. This not only cultivates your own sense of gratitude but also strengthens relationships and creates a positive ripple effect. Who can you call to say "thank you" for their presence in your life or something they have done lately?

Person's name: _____.

I'm grateful for this person because:

_____.

I'm going to call them and tell them this on (day and time):

_____.

In lieu of a call, you could also send a text message, or a letter, if desired. After you reach out to someone and express your gratitude toward them, reflect on the experience: How did it feel to share your gratitude? How did the person react?

_____

_____.

Journaling

Journaling is a powerful tool for processing emotions, gaining perspective, and identifying thought and behavior patterns. It enhances your self-awareness, emotional resilience, and personal growth. Try the following approaches to journaling:

Stream-of-Consciousness Writing

Write down your thoughts about your current financial circumstances. Just write whatever comes to mind, without worrying about grammar or structure. This free-flowing style allows you to express your emotions and uncover deeper feelings.

_____

_____

_____

_____.

Reflective Writing

Now take a more structured approach by analyzing and drawing meaning from your experiences. Reflect on the lessons learned, personal growth, and insights gained from any Dreaded D you've experienced (downsizing, divorce, death of a loved one, disability, disease, disasters, debt, damaged credit, dollar deficits, or discrimination):

_____

_____

_____

_____.

Daily Journaling

To start a journaling habit, aim to dedicate at least 10 minutes a day to writing about your thoughts, feelings, and activities. At the end of the week, reflect on your entries. Did you discover any recurring themes or new insights? Write down your observations here:

_____

_____

_____.

Being Patient with Yourself

Developing resilience takes time and effort. Therefore, you'll need to be patient with yourself and maintain realistic expectations. Two ways to do that are to embrace self-compassion and celebrate small victories along the way. Here's how you can practice patience and self-compassion:

Recognize setbacks as learning opportunities: View setbacks as part of the learning process and understand that progress may not always be linear. Instead of being harsh or critical of yourself during tough times, remind yourself that everyone faces challenges and that growth takes time.

Celebrate small victories: Acknowledge and celebrate your achievements, no matter how minor they may seem. This reinforces your efforts and boosts your confidence, fostering resilience and a positive mindset.

Become a friend to yourself: Reflect on a recent challenge or setback you've faced. How did you respond to it? Were you hard on yourself or did you show patience and understanding? What would you tell a friend who was going through a similar situation? Write your thoughts here:

_____.

Practicing Self-compassion

Self-compassion involves treating yourself with kindness and understanding during adverse circumstances. It allows you to accept and learn from your experiences without becoming overwhelmed by negative emotions. Here's how to practice self-compassion:

Acknowledge your emotions: Be honest with yourself about how you're feeling. Recognize that experiencing a range of emotions, including negative ones, is a natural part of life. Allow yourself to feel and process your emotions without judgment.

Speak kindly to yourself: Replace negative self-talk with compassionate and understanding language. Offer yourself the same words of encouragement and support that you would give to a friend or loved one. Remind yourself that nobody is perfect, and it's normal to face challenges and make mistakes.

Writing Prompt: Choosing Your Words

Consider a recent time you faced a setback or made a mistake. Write down what you said to yourself at that moment. Now, try to rephrase it using kinder, more compassionate language.

Initial thought:

_____.

Rephrased thought:

_____.

Seeking Professional Help

Don't hesitate to seek the guidance of a therapist, counselor, or financial coach if you feel overwhelmed or unable to cope. These professionals can provide support, tools, and strategies to help you navigate challenging situations, process your emotions, and develop coping mechanisms.

Consider the challenges you're currently facing. Do you feel equipped to handle them on your own, or do you think you might benefit from seeking professional help? If you choose to seek help, what type of professional might be best suited to assist you?

Write down your thoughts here and what expertise could be valuable for you: _____

I need help with:	YES	NO
Saving and budgeting	_____	_____
Credit issues	_____	_____
Financial planning	_____	_____
Saving money	_____	_____
Paying off debt	_____	_____
Preparing for retirement	_____	_____

I need help with:	YES	NO
Investing	_____	_____
Estate planning	_____	_____
Taxes	_____	_____
Other issues	_____	_____

Beware These Red Flags with Financial Advisors

One word of caution about hiring a financial advisor—or determining if you should fire a financial advisor. Whether you're looking to hire a financial pro for anything related to investments, or you're on the fence about your current advisor or broker, watch out for red flags that may indicate a potentially problematic advisor. Some red flags to look out for include:

Lack of transparency: Advisors who are not transparent about their fees, commissions, or potential conflicts of interest should be avoided. A trustworthy advisor should clearly explain their compensation structure and disclose any potential conflicts.

Guarantees of specific returns: Financial markets are inherently unpredictable, and no advisor can guarantee specific returns. Be cautious of advisors who promise consistently high returns or claim they can beat the market without fail.

High-pressure sales tactics: Reputable advisors should not pressure you into making decisions quickly or investing in products you don't fully understand. A good advisor will give you time to consider your options and ensure you feel comfortable with your choices.

Lack of proper credentials: A reliable financial advisor should have relevant certifications and qualifications, such as CFP, CFA, or PFS. Be wary of advisors who lack any legitimate credentials or have a history of disciplinary actions.

Unwillingness to customize advice: A good financial advisor should tailor their recommendations to your specific financial situation, goals, and risk tolerance. Be cautious of advisors who offer cookie-cutter solutions or push the same products to all clients.

Limited communication: Advisors who are difficult to reach, unresponsive, or don't communicate in a way that suits your preferences may not be the best fit for you. Effective communication is crucial for a successful advisor-client relationship.

Frequent portfolio turnover: High portfolio turnover can lead to increased trading costs and tax liabilities. Be cautious of advisors who frequently change your investments without clear justification, as this may indicate churning to generate more commissions.

Inadequate documentation: A reputable advisor should provide you with proper documentation, such as written financial plans or regular account statements. A lack of documentation may indicate a lack of organization or transparency.

Too good to be true: If an advisor's claims or promises seem too good to be true, they probably are. Be skeptical of advisors who boast about unrealistic investment returns or downplay the risks associated with their recommendations.

Unregistered firms or advisors: Ensure that the advisor and their firm are registered with the appropriate regulatory bodies, such as FINRA or the SEC. Unregistered advisors may not be subject to the same regulations and standards, increasing the risk of fraud or unethical practices.

By keeping these red flags in mind, you can better protect yourself from unsuitable advisors and increase your chances of finding a reliable and trustworthy financial professional.

Staying Connected

Staying connected with others, especially during challenging times, can help bolster our emotional resilience. It's essential to surround yourself with supportive individuals who can offer both emotional and practical support. Reach out to friends, family, and trusted mentors to discuss your thoughts, worries, and triumphs. Regular connection can help prevent feelings of isolation and can provide a sense of grounding when navigating turbulent periods in life.

Social connection is even more important in the era of digital communication, where we can sometimes feel isolated despite being technologically connected. It's crucial to nurture meaningful relationships that provide mutual support and understanding. Make a conscious effort to stay connected with people who lift you up and provide positive reinforcement.

Put People First

Practice staying connected by being intentional about whom you keep in your inner circle—and who you routinely spend time with. Don't let yourself get too busy to stay in touch. Write down the names of at least three people you can reach out to for emotional support or practical advice. Make a plan to connect with them regularly, whether it's a weekly phone call, a monthly lunch date, or regular messages on social media. Reflect on how these interactions affect your emotional well-being and resilience in the face of financial or personal challenges. Studies show that many US adults don't have a single friend. Bolster your friendships by being proactive.

One long-time friend I'd like to keep up with is:

_____

One new friend or associate I'd like to keep up with is:

_____

One friend of a friend I'd like to get to know better is:

_____

Focusing on Self-care

Self-care is a critical component of resilience, helping us maintain balance in our lives, particularly during stressful times. When we take care of our physical, emotional, and mental well-being, we are better equipped to handle the challenges that come our way. Self-care can include a wide range of activities, from maintaining a healthy diet and regular exercise to practicing mindfulness and pursuing hobbies or activities that bring joy.

Your Self-care Checklist

Identify activities that contribute to your physical, emotional, and mental health. It could be a daily walk, reading a book, practicing yoga, or taking time to meditate. Write down these activities and make a commitment to incorporate them into your daily or weekly routine.

If you're at a loss for ideas, here's a checklist to help you get started:

Self-Care Checklist: 20 Things You Can Do
1. List five things you are grateful for;
2. Listen to your favorite music;

3. Stay off social media;
4. Get extra sleep;
5. Create a travel bucket list;
6. Go for a walk;
7. Try a new hobby or activity;
8. Watch a comedy;
9. Journal;
10. Visit a museum;
11. Soak in a bathtub;
12. Breathe deeply;
13. Watch a sunrise or sunset;
14. Write three things you love about yourself;
15. Exercise;
16. Light some candles;
17. Spend time with supportive family;
18. Stretch your body;
19. Cook your favorite meal;
20. Hug someone.

Additionally, keeping a "Personal Joy Journal" can serve as a powerful reminder of the positive aspects of your life and can encourage you to regularly engage in activities that bring you joy and relaxation. Write down activities you engaged in that brought you happiness or a sense of peace each day for a week. At the end of the week, reflect on the impact of these activities on your mood and resilience. This exercise can help you identify what actions contribute positively to your emotional well-being and encourage you to prioritize them in your life.

Start now by simply listing three things that really make you happy and give you joy:

1. I'm joyful about:

_____.

2. I feel joy when:

_____.

3. _____

_____ also brings me joy.

Establishing a New Money Game Plan

While adjusting to your new financial landscape, it's crucial to devise a strategy that accounts for your revised income and expenses. Here's a step-by-step guide:

Assess your current financial situation: It's time to face your current reality. This is all about getting a handle on your income, expenses, assets, and liabilities. This snapshot will help you grasp your financial standing and highlight areas that need attention.

Create a monthly budget: The cornerstone of financial planning is a well-crafted budget. Use your current assessment to create a realistic budget that outlines all income and expenses. Prioritize essential expenses and consider areas where you can cut back.

Since most people leave out a whole host of categories where they actually spend money, I've found it useful to use a special Budget Worksheet with my clients. Go to this Budget Worksheet in Appendix A. Fill it out to determine whether you have a cash surplus—or if you're in the red monthly.

Reflection questions: When you consider your new budget, what changes do you need to make or what sacrifices might you have to make? How do you feel about that?

_____.

Reflection questions: Looking at your current financial situation, what surprises you the most? Is there something you thought was better or worse than it appears?

_____.

Set financial goals: Once you understand your current financial status, define your short-term and long-term financial goals. These should be in line with your new circumstances.

Short-term Financial Goal Worksheet

GOAL

What is the specific goal? (Be specific and concise)

_____

What is the time frame to accomplish this goal?

_____

What are the metrics that will show your progress?

_____

PURPOSE

Why is this goal important?

_____

What is the benefit of this goal?

_____

CHALLENGES

What obstacles will have to be overcome?

_____

What support, skills, or resources will be needed?

_____

Description of Action Steps	Start Date	Completion Date
_____	_____	_____
_____	_____	_____
_____	_____	_____

Metrics to Track Progress Date	Metrics to Track Progress Date
_____	_____
_____	_____
_____	_____

Long-term Financial Goals Worksheet

GOAL   What is the specific goal? (Be specific and concise)

_____

What is the time frame to accomplish this goal?

_____

What are the metrics that will show your progress?

_____

_____

PURPOSE   Why is this goal important?

_____

What is the benefit of this goal?

_____

CHALLENGES   What obstacles will have to be overcome?

_____

What support, skills, or resources will be needed?

_____

Description of Action Steps	Start Date	Completion Date
_____	_____	_____
_____	_____	_____
_____	_____	_____

Metrics to Track Progress Date	Metrics to Track Progress Date
_____	_____
_____	_____
_____	_____

Reflection questions: How have your financial goals shifted because of your recent challenges? Are there goals that seem more important now than before?

Regularly check your net worth: This is determined by adding up all your assets and then subtracting all your liabilities. In other words, your net worth is everything you *own* minus everything you *owe*. It's a key indicator of financial health and should be monitored regularly to track progress.

Use the Net Worth Worksheet in Appendix B to calculate your net worth.

Reflection question: How does calculating your net worth make you feel? What did you learn from this exercise?

Seek professional guidance: Navigating complex financial decisions can be challenging. Professionals such as financial advisors, accountants, or attorneys can provide expert guidance.

Reflection questions: Have you ever sought professional financial help before? If not, what's holding you back?

I have never asked a financial pro for help because

_____.

I have sought financial expertise and here's what happened:

_____.

Stay proactive and adaptable: Your financial situation can change, and being proactive is crucial. Stay informed, be open to adjustments, and seize new opportunities as they arise.

Reflection questions: How do you typically react to changes in your financial circumstances? How can you be more proactive?

_____

_____.

Maintain open communication with loved ones: If you share finances with others, it's important to communicate openly about financial goals and expectations.

Reflection questions: How comfortable are you discussing financial matters with loved ones? If discomfort exists, how can you work toward open and honest communication?

_____

_____.

Creating a Financial Plan B

Building a contingency plan is crucial for maintaining financial resilience. Consider potential setbacks and devise strategies to address them. Here are steps to create a comprehensive financial plan B:

Identify potential risks and setbacks: List possible events that could adversely affect your finances. Acknowledge these risks to develop tailored strategies and foster preparedness.

Reflection question: Which potential financial risks concern you most, and why?

Evaluate your emergency fund: Aim to save three to six months' worth of living expenses in a readily accessible account. Start slowly if necessary, and build over time.

Reflection question: How prepared are you for a financial emergency?

Review your insurance coverage: Ensure you have sufficient health, life, disability, and property coverage. If there are gaps, consider purchasing additional coverage. Regularly review your policies to stay protected.

Reflection question: Are there areas in your insurance coverage that make you feel vulnerable?

Diversify your income streams: Relying solely on one income source can be risky. Explore ways to create multiple income streams.

Reflection question: How can you diversify your income to reduce reliance on a single source?

Create a plan for each scenario: Devise strategies to address financial implications for each potential setback. Each potential setback requires a unique response strategy. Consider solutions such as cutting expenses, tapping into emergency funds, relying on insurance benefits, or leveraging diversified income sources.

Reflection question: How confident are you in your ability to handle each identified risk?

Maintain a flexible budget: Build flexibility into your budget to accommodate unexpected changes in income or expenses.

Reflection question: How flexible is your current budget?

Review and update your plan regularly: Revisit and update your plan B as your financial situation and priorities change.

Reflection question: How can you ensure regular reviews and updates of your financial plans?

Additional Reflection Questions

What are some of the significant hurdles or obstacles you have faced in your life, whether financial or personal? How did you respond to these challenges?

_____

_____

_____.

Have you noticed any recurring patterns or habits that have hindered your progress or contributed to the difficulties you've encountered?

_____

_____

_____.

Are there any specific beliefs, mindsets, or attitudes that have held you back from bouncing back effectively? How have they influenced your actions or decisions? _____

_____.

Can you identify any past actions or choices that may have contributed to the challenges you're currently facing? What lessons can you learn from those experiences? _____.

As we conclude this second chapter of *The Bounce Back Workbook*, which focused on building your resilience, take time to think about what you have just done, felt, and discovered. What emotions surfaced for you during the exercises? What lessons have you learned so far, and what growth have you experienced? Write a recap below.

_____

_____

Remember, these exercises, reflections, and strategies are tools you can return to again and again to foster resilience. Consistency is key in developing and nurturing resilience, so try to incorporate these practices into your daily life. They can provide valuable insights into your emotions and reactions, help you cultivate gratitude and mindfulness, and ultimately enhance your resilience in the face of adversity. Realize also that it's not about perfection but rather progress. As you continue to practice these strategies, you'll keep building your emotional resilience and improving your ability to bounce back from life's setbacks.

Chapter 3

Downsized from a Job

Losing a job due to downsizing can be a devastating experience that impacts not only your financial stability but also your emotional well-being. In this chapter, we'll explore the challenges that come with downsizing to help you better recover from this difficult scenario. Whether you're dealing with the shock of job loss, grappling with negative emotions, or searching for new employment opportunities, this chapter will provide guidance and hands-on activities to help you bounce back stronger. I've broken this chapter into three sections, based on the advice of experts who recommend that you tend to your emotional well-being first, before you start gearing up for a job search and looking for new employment. The three sections are "Understanding and Processing Job Loss," "Preparing for the Job Search," and "Initiating a Job Search."

Understanding and Processing Job Loss

Change, especially unexpected change, can bring a whirlwind of emotions. Losing your job is no exception. The shock, disbelief, and stress can be overwhelming. Instead, getting laid off can serve as a unique opportunity for self-reflection, skill enhancement, and career reinvention. It might even lead to opportunities and situations that you never expected. At the end of this chapter, I'll tell you why getting laid off turned out to be the best thing that ever happened to me—even though I initially thought it was horribly unfair!

Job loss isn't a reflection of your worth or abilities. Nonetheless, job loss can often feel personal and disheartening. But the truth is layoffs or downsizing are usually strategic business decisions made due to external factors such as economic conditions, company restructuring, or changes in business direction. Being let go is not an indication of your capabilities or value. Keeping this idea in mind will help you better navigate your emotions.

Whatever range of emotions you experience after job loss is natural. Give yourself the space and time to grieve and adjust. Acknowledge your feelings, whether they're anger, sadness, anxiety, or even relief. Then strive to express these emotions constructively: anything from writing in this *Workbook*, talking to a supportive friend, or seeking professional counseling if necessary.

Reflection questions:

How did you feel when you first learned about the downsizing?

_____

_____.

What are the dominant emotions you're feeling right now?

_____

_____.

How have your feelings about being terminated changed over time?

_____

_____.

What methods can you adopt to express your emotions healthily?

_____

_____.

What coping mechanisms have helped you navigate these emotions?

_____

_____.

Reflecting on the Psychological Contract

In *Bounce Back*, I explained the concept of the psychological contract, which is the unwritten agreement that employees and employers have about the expectations, understandings, and informal commitments that govern their working relationship. Take time now to reflect on your own expectations and beliefs about your previous employer and the employment relationship. Consider the following questions:

What were your expectations regarding job security, career development, work-life balance, and fair treatment in your previous job?

_____

_____

_____.

How did the layoff disrupt or contradict these expectations? How did it impact your trust and loyalty toward the organization?

_____

_____.

Are there any lessons or insights you can draw from this experience to shape your expectations in future employment relationships?

_____

_____.

Seeking Support and Sharing Your Story

One way to better process your feelings about job loss is to reach out to trusted friends, family members, or support groups to discuss your emotions and experiences. Share your story with them and listen to their stories in return. Supportive individuals can provide guidance, encouragement, and accountability as you navigate your career transition. Use the following questions as thought starters and answer them honestly:

How have your relationships with others been affected by your job loss?

_____

_____.

How have their support and understanding helped you navigate this difficult period?

_____

_____.

In what ways have family and friends been helpful or not helpful during this time?

_____

_____.

Have you discovered any new insights or perspectives through sharing your story with others?

_____

_____.

How has this impacted your healing process?

_____

_____.

How do you typically cope with difficult emotions?

_____

_____.

What healthy or unhealthy patterns have you noticed?

_____

_____.

Creating Some Me-time

One additional strategy for dealing with job loss is to really focus on taking care of yourself, physically and emotionally. When you're not working, keeping a healthy outlooking can be enhanced in many ways. But two techniques, in particular, can offer an emotional pick me up.

Self-care rituals: Establish self-care rituals that nurture your emotional well-being. This could include activities such as taking walks in nature, practicing yoga, listening to music, or engaging in creative pursuits. When designing a self-care routine, identify activities that bring you joy and relaxation. For some people, it's hobbies, exercises, or practices such as meditation, journaling, or gardening. Schedule regular self-care time in your daily or weekly routine. Experiment with different self-care practices and find what works best for you. Everyone's needs are different, so explore a variety of activities and customize your routine accordingly. Take note also of how incorporating self-care into your routine impacts your over-all well-being. Notice any positive changes in your mood, stress levels, or resilience.

Supportive affirmations: Develop a list of affirmations or positive statements that you can repeat to yourself during challenging moments. For example, "I am resilient and capable of overcoming obstacles," or "I embrace uncertainty as an opportunity for growth."

If you find it very hard to say any positive words to yourself, use this as a chance to go deeper. Ask yourself the following questions and write the answers that ring true for you.

Reflection questions:

Have you allowed yourself to fully process your emotions around the layoff, or have you been suppressing them? If so, why?

_____

_____

_____.

How has job loss impacted your self-esteem and sense of self-worth? To what extent was your identity tied to your title, former role, or employer?

_____

_____

_____.

Are there any activities or practices that have helped you cope with the emotional challenges of job loss? If yes, what are they? If not, are there any strategies you'd like to explore?

_____

_____.

Reviewing Your Former Job and Soul Searching for Your Next Ideal Job

As a final part of understanding your needs and emotions in the wake of job loss, I want you to reflect on both the good and the bad aspects of your past job, as well as engage in a soul-searching exercise to identify what you truly want in your next job or career. Use the following prompts to guide your reflection:

Instructions: Read the following statements, think about your past job, and check whether each statement was true or false for you.

The Truth About My Old Job

	T	F
I had a good work-life balance.		
I was well paid based on my work experience and background in the industry.		
My efforts and contributions were recognized and honored.		
I liked my coworkers.		
I liked my bosses.		
I had the type of flexibility I needed or desired.		
I enjoyed the work I performed.		
I was not overworked.		
I was able to advance and earn promotions.		
I had opportunities to learn new things.		
I was excited and happy to go to work.		
I found meaning or purpose in my work.		

Take a look at how many TRUE responses you selected. What did you notice in your answers? Was the job all that you wanted in an ideal world?

Now imagine waving a magic wand and getting *exactly* what you want in a job. What does that look like? Consider factors such as salary, work-life balance, skills utilized, purpose, impact, creativity, and any other aspects that are important to you. Reflect again on your past experiences.

What were the best aspects of your previous job or career?

_____

_____.

What were the areas that you didn't enjoy or would not want to carry forward?

_____.

Now write out your ideal job description, incorporating all the elements that you have identified. Don't limit yourself based on what you think is feasible or has been done before. Dream big and be creative in envisioning your ideal role.

_____

_____

_____

_____.

Building a Strong Financial Foundation

Now that you've addressed some of the emotional aspects of job loss, you can start tending to financial matters. You'll want to assess your economic situation by first listing all sources of income you may have, including severance packages, unemployment benefits, or anything else.

Next, it's important to evaluate your expenses and prioritize them based on necessity. If you've recently lost your job, or have not yet found employment, it's wise to identify areas where you can cut back or reduce spending temporarily. You never know exactly how long it will take to find a new position. So it's better safe than sorry when it comes to spending decisions. This will put you in the right mindset to do what is ultimately necessary: creating a revised budget.

Developing a Layoff Survival Budget

After a layoff, it's advisable to develop a new budget that aligns with your changed financial circumstances. Don't just look at income and expenses. Take inventory of your assets and savings too, including any emergency funds or retirement accounts—though the latter should only be tapped as a last resort. Are your resources or reserves sufficient to support you during your job search? If not, what steps can you take to build or maintain your emergency fund?

Once you've considered the items mentioned here, it's time to think about your monthly budget. To guide your budgeting process, categorize your expenses into essential and nonessential categories. Allocate your available income accordingly, ensuring that essential expenses are covered first. Explore opportunities to reduce costs, such as negotiating bills, switching to more affordable alternatives, or eliminating discretionary expenses. If you've previously been saving money, try not to stop saving altogether. Set realistic savings goals based on your revised income. Even small contributions to savings can help build financial resilience over time.

Regularly review and adjust your budget as needed to accommodate changes in your financial situation.

Maximizing Benefits and Assistance Programs

To help tide you over financially, don't hesitate to take advantage of any benefits you're entitled to from your former employer. Also, don't be shy about leveraging assistance programs, such as unemployment, that can support you during this period. Get ideas from this checklist and following suggested action steps:

Checklist and Action Steps for Financial Benefits and Support
- ✓ Create a list of any and all termination benefits my former employer offered (this could be résumé service, career coaching, and more);
- ✓ Investigate unemployment benefits in my state;
- ✓ Determine my unemployment eligibility;
- ✓ Understand the application process and necessary documentation;
- ✓ Review my health insurance options;
- ✓ Evaluate coverage alternatives, such as COBRA or marketplace plans;
- ✓ Research programs that offer job search support or skill-building opportunities.

If you are anticipating a layoff, or are in the middle of negotiating your departure terms, you can also ask for the most possible support from your job. When employers terminate employees, they may offer various benefits as part of the termination package. Here are 10 potential benefits employers may offer:

Checklist of Items to Request Prior to or During a Termination

Severance pay: Employers may provide a lump sum or ongoing payments to employees as compensation for the termination. The amount is often based on factors such as length of service and position held.

Requested?   YES or NO

Extended health insurance: Employers may offer continued health insurance coverage for a specified period after termination. This can provide valuable peace of mind for employees during the transition period.

Requested?   YES or NO

Outplacement services: Some companies offer outplacement services, which provide support to terminated employees in finding new job opportunities. This may include career counseling, résumé writing assistance, and job search resources.

Requested?   YES or NO

Extended employment benefits: Employers may extend certain employment benefits beyond the termination date. For example, employees may continue to receive their usual vacation accrual, access to employee discounts, or retirement plan contributions for a specific period.

Requested?   YES or NO

Retraining or education assistance: To help terminated employees enhance their skills and increase employability, employers may provide financial support or access to training programs or educational courses.

Requested?   YES or NO

Reference letters: Employers may offer to provide reference letters or act as a reference for terminated employees during their job search. Positive references can significantly impact an employee's ability to secure future employment. Requested? YES or NO

Career transition assistance: Companies may provide career transition services, such as workshops or coaching sessions, to help terminated employees explore new career paths, improve interview skills, and develop job search strategies. Requested? YES or NO

Job placement support: In some cases, employers may leverage their networks and connections to assist terminated employees in finding new job opportunities. This can involve introductions to potential employers or assistance with job placement agencies. Requested? YES or NO

Extended access to company resources: Employees may be granted temporary access to company resources, such as email or online training platforms, to aid in their job search or professional development. Requested? YES or NO

Non-compete or non-disclosure waivers: Employers may release employees from previously signed agreements, in effect waiving former non-compete or non-disclosure clauses. This allows employees to seek employment with competitors or share their experiences without legal restrictions. Requested? YES or NO

Getting Temporary, Freelance, or Gig Work

If you find yourself in need of income during your job search, consider exploring freelance or gig work opportunities. Follow these steps:

Identify your skills and areas of expertise that can be utilized in a freelance capacity. Think about the services you can offer on a project basis. Research online platforms and job boards that connect freelancers with clients seeking their services. Examples include Upwork, Freelancer, Fiverr, and Gigster.

Create a compelling freelance profile or portfolio that showcases your skills, experience, and previous work. Start bidding or applying for freelance projects that align with your skills and interests. Tailor your proposals to highlight your unique value proposition. Also, continue to network with professionals in your desired industry or field to uncover freelance opportunities through referrals or recommendations.

Stay organized and manage your time effectively to balance your job search activities with your freelance work commitments.

Exploring Interim Economic Moves

After you leave your former place of employment and before you find the ideal new job, you may need to take some intermediate steps to stay in the black. Consider the interim economic moves mentioned in *Bounce Back* and evaluate their feasibility for your situation. Reflect on the following questions:

What consulting, freelance, or gig opportunities align with your skills and interests?

_____.

How can you leverage those opportunities while searching for a full-time job?

_____.

Have you considered part-time or temporary employment to provide financial stability during your job search? Why or why not?

_____.

What industries or positions could be a good fit for you?

_____

_____.

Preparing for the Job Search

When you're emotionally ready and you've addressed your immediate financial needs, it's time to consider what the future of employment looks like for you. Not just any old job but a position that brings you fulfillment and what you desire—on your terms. To best prepare yourself, use this transition period to reassess your career goals. Reflect on what you enjoyed about your past job, the skills you have, the work culture you thrive in, and the kind of job you'd like to have. Consider your long-term career trajectory, work-life balance, and personal growth opportunities.

Reflection questions:

What are the key takeaways from your previous job?

_____

_____

_____

How do your career aspirations align with your life goals?

_____

_____

_____

What are the nonnegotiables in your future job?

_____

_____

_____

Identifying Transferable Skills and Strengths

In preparation for a new role, be prepared to think outside the box—or in this case, outside your prior industry. There's no rule that says you have to keep working in the exact same sector or industry that you did before. Explore your transferable skills and strengths that can be applied to different industries or job roles. Taking the following action steps will help:

Action Steps to Identify Transferable Skills
✓ Make a list of your core skills and competencies developed throughout your career.

✓ Reflect on the experiences and achievements that highlight these skills.
✓ Research various industries that align with your passions, interests, and values.
✓ Identify industries or roles where your transferable skills can be valuable.

Upgrading Your Skill Set

Identify skills required in your target job market and determine if you need to upgrade your existing skill set. Utilize online platforms, professional courses, or workshops to learn and enhance your skills. This not only boosts your employability but also fosters personal growth.

If there are specific skills or certifications that are in high demand in your target industries, consider pursuing additional training or certifications to enhance your qualifications and increase your marketability. Volunteering or taking on apprenticeships and internships can be valuable too. These experiences can provide you with hands-on experience, expand your network, and demonstrate your commitment to learning and adapting to a new field.

Reflection questions:

What skills are currently in demand in your industry?

_____

_____

_____.

What are your existing strengths and areas for improvement?

_____

_____

_____.

What learning resources can you utilize to upgrade your skills?

_____.

What would you need to learn to do if you wanted to switch industries?

_____

_____

_____.

Building a Supportive Job Search Network

Expanding and strengthening your professional network will enhance your job search efforts.

So get ready to reach out to former colleagues, supervisors, mentors, and industry contacts to inform them of your job search and ask for their assistance or referrals. Be prepared to attend industry events, conferences, or webinars to meet new professionals and expand your network. Join professional associations or online communities related to your target industry to connect with like-minded individuals and access job opportunities. Begin now by listing three industry contacts/former colleagues, three family members, and three friends who could be helpful in some way in your upcoming job hunt.

My Network
1. Industry contact _____
2. Industry contact _____
3. Industry contact _____
4. Family member _____
5. Family member _____
6. Family member _____
7. Friend _____
8. Friend _____
9. Friend _____

Polishing Your Résumé and LinkedIn Profile

There are many ways you can enhance your résumé and LinkedIn profile in preparation for your job hunt and outreach to prospective employers.

Start by reviewing your existing résumé and updating it with your most recent experience, skills, and accomplishments. Remove any irrelevant information or outdated job details. Tailor your résumé for each job application by highlighting the skills and experiences that are most relevant to the specific position you're applying for. Proofread your résumé carefully for spelling and grammatical errors. Consider asking a trusted friend or family member to review it as well.

Your updated LinkedIn profile should align with your résumé. Use a professional headshot, write a compelling summary, and list your relevant skills and experiences. Be sure to request recommendations from former colleagues, supervisors, or clients to strengthen your profile. It doesn't hurt to also engage with LinkedIn groups and share relevant articles or insights to demonstrate your expertise and engage with professionals in your industry.

Finally, use action verbs and quantifiable achievements to make your résumé more impactful. For example, instead of saying "responsible for managing a team," say "successfully led a team of 10 employees, resulting in a 20% increase in productivity."

Case Study: Résumé and LinkedIn Profile Enhancement

Ervin Johnson, a mid-level executive who bounced back quickly from a downsizing, also recommends incorporating keywords from the job description into your résumé to improve its visibility to applicant tracking systems. He says this technique helped him tremendously. "My résumé is much tighter than it's ever been. The words on there really matter because they show up in keyword searches." A native of North Carolina who now lives in Washington, DC, Johnson formerly worked for a consumer products company before a corporate reorganization eliminated his position and many others in the spring of 2023. Johnson had a nice severance package, for which he said he was grateful. But he also emphasized the strategic nature of his search and a few insider tips about using LinkedIn.

"I just didn't apply for random jobs. This was a purpose-driven search, so it made the search much more stress-free," Johnson says. One of his tips: get LinkedIn premium, because it's worth it. As of this writing, the premium service cost $39.99 per month. But Johnson swears by it. "With LinkedIn Premium, when I applied for a job, I could see how many applicants have applied. I could see a skill comparison between me and other candidates. And it even spits out your chance of getting an interview or if you're a top applicant. That's very valuable," he said.

Perhaps most important, though, Johnson said that when you apply for jobs via LinkedIn Premium, the service emails you back and shows you exactly who looked at your emailed application. Whenever Johnson got an email from LinkedIn indicating who the person was that reviewed his initial email, he would then find the person on LinkedIn and reach out directly to them. That nudge proved powerful.

"Just by doing that, I got a lot of responses back from hiring managers and that got me pushed through to recruiters at different organizations," Johnson says, adding that without the email of a specific hiring manager, job applicants are often applying in the dark or don't know precisely when someone has reviewed their materials.

Johnson said his efforts over two months yielded him about 16 first-round interviews and eight company interviews where he progressed along the interview process to the next round. He ultimately landed a good offer with a science research firm where he's developing partnerships to advance health equity.

Initiating the Job Search

Once your résumé and LinkedIn profile are in tip-top shape, it's time to pull out all the stops in your quest for the right position. At this phase, you'll want to create a networking action plan, conduct informational interviews, hone your interviewing skills, and generally polish up your presentation skills and social outreach in order to put your best foot forward.

Creating a Networking Action Plan

Networking is a valuable tool in your job search and can provide support and opportunities for new employment. You can expand and maintain your professional network in a variety of ways.

Reach out to former colleagues, friends, and family members to inform them of your job search and ask for their support or referrals. Join professional associations or industry-specific groups related to your field of interest. Attend their events, conferences, or webinars to connect with professionals in your industry. Utilize online networking platforms such as LinkedIn to connect with individuals who work in your desired field or industry. Send personalized messages to introduce yourself and express your interest in connecting. Participate in job search groups or support groups where you can share experiences, insights, and job leads with others in a similar situation.

Stay connected with individuals outside of the job world as well. Maintain relationships with friends, family, and mentors who can provide emotional support and perspective during your job search.

Take advantage of networking opportunities in your community too, such as local business events, volunteer activities, or informational interviews with professionals in your target industry. Follow up with individuals you meet during networking activities. Send thank-you notes or emails expressing your appreciation for their time and insights. By engaging in these activities and exercises, you will be better equipped to navigate the emotional, financial, and practical aspects of job loss. Remember to be patient with yourself, prioritize self-care, and approach your job search with a proactive and strategic mindset.

To create an effective networking action plan, follow these steps: First, identify your networking goals. What do you hope to achieve through networking? Examples could include finding job leads, gaining industry insights, or expanding your professional contacts. Make a list of individuals in your network that you want to reach out to, including former colleagues, friends, family members, and industry professionals. Set specific networking goals, such as reaching out to a certain number of people per week or attending a certain number of networking events per month. Determine the best methods for connecting with your network, whether it's through email, LinkedIn messages, phone calls, or in-person meetings.

Craft personalized messages when reaching out to individuals, expressing your interest in connecting and mentioning any specific ways in which they can help or provide support.

Follow up with individuals after networking interactions, expressing gratitude for their time and insights. Regularly update your network on your job search progress and any relevant achievements or milestones. Be proactive in offering support and assistance to your network as well. Networking is a two-way street, and building mutually beneficial relationships is key.

By implementing these activities and strategies, you'll maximize your chances of finding new employment and successfully navigating the job market after a layoff. Remember to stay proactive, persistent, and positive throughout the process.

Reflection questions:

What professional associations or industry-specific groups can I join to expand my network?

_____

_____.

What local networking opportunities exist in my community?

_____

_____.

How can I offer support and assistance to my network while seeking their
    help?

_____

_____.

What fears or concerns do I have about networking, and how can I
    address them?

_____

_____.

If I'm anxious in any way about networking, how can I reframe my per-
    spective on the process to see it as an opportunity for connection and
    growth rather than a daunting task?

_____

_____.

If you struggle with networking, reflect on any fears or concerns you have,
such as fear of rejection, feeling like a burden, or not knowing what to say.
Explore ways to address these concerns, such as practicing self-compassion,
reminding yourself of your value and skills, and preparing talking points or
elevator pitches to feel more confident in networking interactions.

Additionally, consider how you currently perceive networking and
whether any negative beliefs or assumptions are holding you back. Reflect
on how reframing your perspective on networking as an opportunity for
connection, learning, and personal growth can help alleviate anxieties
and motivate you to engage in networking activities with a more positive
mindset.

Conducting Informational Interviews

Take the research phase of your job search seriously by conducting informational interviews with professionals in the industry or role you are interested in. Follow these steps:

Identify individuals who work in the field or job function you are considering. You can reach out to your existing network, use professional networking platforms such as LinkedIn, or join relevant industry groups or events. Request informational interviews with these individuals. Explain that you are exploring new career opportunities and would like to learn more about their experiences and insights.

Prepare a list of questions to ask during the informational interview. Inquire about their day-to-day responsibilities, career path, challenges, and any advice they have for someone looking to enter the field. Actively listen and take notes during the informational interviews. Use this opportunity to gain a realistic understanding of the job or career path, gather valuable insights, and expand your professional network.

Checklist: Enhancing Your Interview Techniques

To improve your interview techniques and increase your chances of success, focus on the following checklist of activities:

✓ Practice answering common interview questions, particularly behavioral questions that require you to provide specific examples from your past experiences.
✓ Work on improving your communication skills, including clarity, conciseness, and effective storytelling.
✓ Develop a list of insightful questions to ask during interviews to demonstrate your interest in the company and the position.
✓ Consider participating in mock interviews with a career coach, mentor, or trusted friend who can provide feedback and help you refine your responses.
✓ Continuously work on building confidence and maintaining a positive attitude during interviews. Confidence in your abilities will help you make a lasting impression on interviewers.

Reflecting on Interview Experiences and Improving

Reflect on your interview experiences and analyze areas where you can improve your performance. Consider the following questions:

How did you feel during the interview process?   _____
Were there any specific moments or questions   _____
that you found challenging?

Evaluate your communication skills during   YES or NO
the interview. Did you confidently respond to
behavioral questions and provide solid examples
of your abilities?

Assess your level of engagement and profession-   YES or NO
alism throughout the entire interview process.
Did you maintain enthusiasm and effectively
demonstrate your interest in the position, particularly if there were multiple rounds of interviews with an employer?

If you had a good connection with any interviewers, consider reaching out and requesting feedback on your application and interview. Their insights can provide valuable guidance for refining your interview techniques.

Making Informed Decisions on Job Offers

When considering job offers, make sure to carefully evaluate whether they align with your needs and aspirations. Use the following steps to guide your decision-making process:

Reflect on your wants and needs in your next job. Consider factors such as work-life balance, growth opportunities, company culture, and alignment with your long-term career goals. Review the earlier activity entitled "The Truth about My Old Job" and examine the "True" and "False" statements you checked, and the answers you wrote down about what you do want and don't want in a job.

Take your time to assess the job offer and compare it to your desired criteria. Ask yourself:

✓ Does the job offer provide the salary and benefits I require?
✓ Does the company culture align with my values and work style?

✓ Are there opportunities for growth and development?
✓ Does the position offer the work-life balance I seek?
✓ Will accepting the job move me closer to my long-term career goals?
✓ Are there any red flags or concerns that need to be addressed?

Consider the potential long-term impact of accepting the job offer. Think about how it aligns with your overall career trajectory and whether it will contribute positively to your professional growth.

If you're unsure about accepting an offer, don't rush your decision. Give yourself enough time to weigh the pros and cons, and seek advice from trusted mentors or career professionals.

Exploring Entrepreneurship

If you find yourself considering entrepreneurship as an alternative to finding another job, take the following steps to explore this option further:

Self-reflection: Reflect on your interests, passions, and skills. Consider what type of business or industry aligns with your strengths and values. Ask yourself what you truly enjoy doing and what problems you would like to solve through your business.

Research: Conduct thorough market research to identify potential opportunities and assess the viability of your business idea. Explore the market demand, competition, target audience, and potential challenges you may face.

Business planning: Develop a comprehensive business plan that outlines your vision, mission, target market, products or services, marketing strategy, financial projections, and operational details. This plan will serve as a road map for your entrepreneurial journey.

Seek guidance: Connect with experienced entrepreneurs, join entrepreneurial communities or organizations, and seek mentorship to gain insights and advice from those who have already embarked on a similar path. Their guidance can help you navigate the challenges and increase your chances of success.

Acquire knowledge and skills: If you lack experience in running a business, consider taking relevant courses, attending workshops, or pursuing entrepreneurship programs to acquire the necessary knowledge and skills. This will help you develop a strong foundation and increase your confidence in managing your own venture.

Start small: Consider starting your business as a side project while you are still exploring the entrepreneurial path. This will allow you to test the market, refine your products or services, and gain experience without fully committing your time and resources.

Take action: Once you have done your research, developed a business plan, and acquired the necessary skills, it's time to take the leap and launch your business. Stay focused, be adaptable, and embrace the challenges and learning opportunities that come your way.

Small business owners know that entrepreneurship is a journey that requires perseverance, resilience, and continuous learning. It may not be easy, but with dedication and a clear vision, you can create a successful and fulfilling venture.

Reflection questions:

What aspects of entrepreneurship or nontraditional careers resonate with you the most? Why?

_____

_____

_____.

What skills and experiences do you already possess that can be transferred to these alternative career paths?

_____

_____.

What specific steps can you take to explore entrepreneurship or nontraditional careers further?

_____

_____.

How can you leverage your existing network or expand your connections to gain insights and opportunities in these fields?

_____

_____.

What challenges do you anticipate in pursuing entrepreneurship, and how
can you overcome them?

_____

_____.

How does pursuing entrepreneurship or a nontraditional career align with
your long-term goals and aspirations?

_____

_____.

How can you maintain a balance between taking calculated risks and
ensuring financial stability during this transition?

_____

_____.

What research and exploration have you conducted regarding entrepreneurship and the specific industry or business idea you're considering?

_____

_____.

Have you sought advice or mentorship from experienced entrepreneurs or
professionals to gain insights and guidance? Why or why not?

_____

_____.

How does the concept of a "blessing in disguise" resonate with you in rela-
tion to your job loss and potential entrepreneurial path?

_____

_____.

Take the time to reflect on these questions and use the answers as a guide
to make informed decisions about your career path. Remember, there is no
one-size-fits-all answer, and it's important to choose the path that is best
based on your unique situation.

Getting Fired Was a Big Blessing

In my case, entrepreneurship was absolutely the right choice. In fact, leaving our jobs—one voluntarily, the other *not* voluntarily—is what brought my husband, Earl, and I together.

Earl previously worked for John Wiley & Sons, the company that is the publisher of this book and *Bounce Back*. Wiley is one of the world's largest publishers of business and nonfiction books. In 2002, while Earl was employed at Wiley, he also had a side gig—publishing works of fiction for authors and helping them promote those books. Earl told his bosses about his extra stream of income, and all was well until one day that year, one of his bosses confronted him and gave him an ultimatum: he told Earl to choose between keeping his side hustle or keeping his main job. Earl chose his side hustle and turned it into a full-time gig as a business owner, publisher, book agent, and consultant to authors. He left Wiley in July 2002. The next year, in June 2003, Earl went to an industry conference called Book Expo in Los Angeles to network and pick up clients—and to show his old boss that he was doing just fine and thriving, in fact, working for himself.

It turns out that I attended that same Book Expo conference in 2003. Wiley—Earl's former company—had made me an offer to buy my first book, called *Investing Success*. I initially said yes to their offer. But when I was terminated along with 200 other people from Dow Jones—and I lost my job as a *Wall Street Journal* reporter for CNBC in March 2003—I had a change of heart. I decided to self-publish *Investing Success* and start my own business.

At Book Expo, I delivered the news to Wiley executives, and they graciously understood. But a woman named Michelle Patterson, who was then a marketing manager at Wiley, pulled me to the side and referred me to Earl. She said if I was going to self-publish I should at least have a book industry expert who could help me navigate the process. Earl and I would meet later at the conclusion of Book Expo—at the airport, coincidentally—after a red-eye flight back from LA to New Jersey. During our very first conversation, Earl told me that he was impressed that I wrote an investing book, but perhaps I should write about credit card debt since so many folks were mired in debt. "You write a book teaching people how to get out of debt, and that'll become a *New York Times* bestseller," Earl said. He was spot on. My second book was *Zero Debt: The Ultimate Guide to Financial Freedom*, and it hit the *New York Times* bestseller's list.

Who knew that us both leaving "good" jobs would lead us to the best roles of all—as happily married spouses, parents to three great kids, and entrepreneurs who have worked together in business now for two decades? None of that would have happened if we stayed at our former employers. So that's why I now say that getting fired was one of the best things to ever happen to me!

As we conclude this third chapter of *The Bounce Back Workbook*, which focused on being downsized from a job, take time to think about what you have just done, felt, and discovered. What emotions surfaced for you during the exercises? What lessons have you learned so far, and what growth have you experienced? Write a recap below.

_____

_____

_____

_____

Chapter 4

Divorce

Divorce is a major life transition that brings about a huge number of challenges, emotions, and potential financial issues. It can be depressing or liberating, depending on your outlook. It's also a time of reflection, healing, and rebuilding. In this chapter, we'll look at the emotional aspects of divorce and how to navigate the complex terrain of disentangling your finances from your ex. With the right mindset and support, and by embracing emotional healing and financial empowerment, you can create a strong foundation for your post-divorce life. Breaking up doesn't have to break you. Even though it may not initially seem like it, the next phase of life could become one of your biggest periods of self-discovery, independence, and emotional resilience.

Throughout this chapter, give your best effort to really work through the suggested exercises, fill-in-the-blank questions, activities, writing prompts, and case studies in order for you to reflect on and explore your experiences and emotions related to divorce.

Emotional Healing and Taking an Honest Look at What Went Wrong

Divorce often prompts us to reevaluate our expectations and beliefs about marriage, or about relationships and people in general. Take a moment to reflect on your own expectations before your divorce. How did these expectations shape your experience, and how can you redefine them moving forward? Consider the following questions and then write down key lessons you learned from your previous marriage that will help you navigate future relationships.

Reflection questions:

Take a moment to reflect on your own expectations and beliefs about marriage before your divorce. What did you think marriage would be like before you walked down the aisle?

_____

_____.

How did these expectations play out in your marriage?

_____

_____.

How have your expectations about marriage evolved through your divorce experience?

_____

_____.

What insights have you gained about yourself and your relationships during this process?

_____

_____.

Write down three key lessons you learned from your previous marriage and your breakup that will help you navigate future relationships.

Lesson #1: _____

Lesson #2: _____

Lesson #3: _____

How can you apply these lessons in your actions to foster healthier relationships in the future?

_____

_____.

Evaluating Compatibility and Growth

Every divorce has unique circumstances and challenges. Reflect on your past relationship and identify the factors that contributed to its incompatibility. Explore the major challenges you faced during your marriage and the important lessons you learned from your divorce. Additionally, consider the qualities you seek in a future partner.

Reflection questions:

Looking back, what were the core reasons for the incompatibility in your previous marriage?

_____

_____

How did the major challenges you faced impact your relationship, and what exactly did you learn from them?

_____

_____

Based on your experiences, what three qualities would you prioritize in a future partner?

Quality #1: _____

This is important to me because: _____

_____

Quality #2: _____

This is important to me because: _____

_____

Quality #3: _____

This is important to me because: _____

_____

Redefining Self-identity and Priorities

Divorce provides an opportunity for self-reflection and personal growth. Take time to reflect on your values, interests, and goals. Write a personal mission statement that captures your vision for your future. Additionally, list three activities or hobbies that bring you joy and allow you to reconnect with yourself. Finally, set three personal goals for the next year that align with your newfound priorities and aspirations.

Reflection questions:

How have your values, interests, and goals shifted during and after the divorce?

How can you integrate your values and passions into your daily life moving forward?

What steps can you take to achieve the personal goals you have set for yourself?

Take time to reflect on your values, interests, and goals. Write a personal mission statement that captures your vision for your future.

This is what I want for my future:

_____

_____

_____.

Additionally, list three activities or hobbies that bring you joy and allow you to reconnect with yourself.

Activity or hobby #1: _____.

Activity or hobby #2: _____.

Activity or hobby #3: _____.

Finally, set three personal goals for the next year that align with your newfound priorities and aspirations.

Goal #1: _____.

Goal #2: _____.

Goal #3: _____.

Processing Emotions and Seeking Support

Divorce can elicit a wide range of emotions, from anger and sadness to relief and uncertainty. It's essential to give yourself the space and time to process these emotions. Explore healthy ways to express and manage your feelings, whether it's through journaling, talking to a supportive friend, exercising, or seeking professional counseling. Identify individuals in your support network who can provide emotional support during this challenging time.

Reflection questions:

What emotions have you been experiencing since the divorce, and how have they impacted your daily life?

_____

_____

_____.

How do you currently cope with these emotions, and are there any new strategies you would like to explore?

_____

_____

_____.

Is there any part of you that is glad to be divorced? Why or why not? Are you feeling relieved or freer in any way? If so, why?

_____

_____

_____

Who are the individuals in your support network that have provided emotional support during your divorce?

_____

_____

_____.

Rebuilding Supportive Relationships

During and after divorce, having a strong support network is crucial. Make a list of people in your support network who have been there for you during and after your divorce. Reach out to one or two individuals on your list and express your gratitude for their support. Consider joining support groups or attending counseling sessions to connect with others who have gone through similar experiences.

Reflection questions:

How have friends, family, or colleagues impacted your healing process, and how can you express your gratitude to them?

_____

_____

_____

What steps can you take to expand your support network and connect with others who understand your experience?

_____

_____

_____

Further Emotional Processing and Healing

Reflect on the emotional impact of the divorce on your self-esteem, self-worth, and identity. How can you separate your sense of self from the dissolution of the marriage and find inner healing and self-acceptance?

_____

_____

_____

Activity: Embracing Self-care and Emotional Well-being

Engage in self-care activities that support your emotional well-being, such as journaling, meditation, exercise, or spending time in nature. Additionally, practice self-compassion, kindness, and understanding to yourself by acknowledging and validating your emotions throughout the divorce journey. These self-care practices will help you process emotions, reduce stress, and cultivate resilience during the divorce recovery process. Finally, identify a support network of friends, family, or support groups who can provide emotional support and understanding. Think about how you can seek and accept help from others without feeling ashamed or isolated.

Casting Off Your Ex-spouse Financially

Just like it can be an emotional ordeal to go through a breakup, recovering from a divorce and disentangling economically from a previous spouse can also be quite a complex process. In this section, we'll look at the first four key steps you need to take to properly separate your finances after divorce and begin rebuilding your own life.

STEP 1. Close joint accounts

Action Step: List Joint Accounts

Take some time to list all the joint bank accounts, credit cards, loans, and other financial accounts that you share with your former spouse. Include checking, savings, and investment accounts, as well as mortgages and car loans.

Type of Financial Account	Institution
Checking account	_____
Savings account	_____
Money market account	_____
Certificate of deposit (CD)	_____
Brokerage account #1	_____
Brokerage account #2	_____
Brokerage account #3	_____
Investment account #1	_____
Investment account #2	_____

Type of Financial Account	Institution
Investment account #3	_____
Credit card #1	_____
Credit card #2	_____
Credit card #3	_____
Credit card #4	_____
Auto loan #1	_____
Auto loan #2	_____
Mortgage	_____
HELOC/Home equity loan	_____
Other loan #1	_____
Other loan #2	_____

Reflection questions:

How do you feel about the process of closing these joint accounts?

What emotions arise when considering the division of assets and liabilities?

How can you approach these discussions with your former spouse or seek assistance from a mediator or attorney to minimize conflicts?

Exercise: Dividing Assets and Liabilities

Based on your divorce settlement, court order, or any preliminary agreements, decide how you will split the assets and liabilities. Consider reaching an agreement with your former spouse and putting it in writing. Seek legal advice if necessary.

STEP 2. Update beneficiaries and estate planning documents

Action Step: Review Beneficiary Designations

Review your retirement accounts, insurance policies, and other financial accounts to determine the designated beneficiaries. Consider whom you want to update as the new beneficiaries, such as your children, a new spouse, or another family member.

Write down who should be the beneficiary or beneficiaries on your retirement plans and life insurance.

Beneficiary #1: _____

Beneficiary #2: _____

Beneficiary #3: _____

Important next task: Contact your employer or life insurance company and request the necessary paperwork to change your beneficiary designations as needed. Don't overlook this step! Give yourself some deadlines to ensure that you don't forget this crucial item.

Deadline Date to Complete Task   Date Task Completed

_____   _____

Action Step: Revise Legal Documents

Review your last will and testament, trust, power of attorney, and advance health care directive. Assess the need to remove your former spouse as a beneficiary, trustee, or agent. Consult with an estate planning attorney to ensure proper revisions.

STEP 3. Change your name if applicable, and if desired

Action Step: Obtain Legal Documentation

Obtain a certified copy of your divorce decree or court order stating your name change. This will serve as legal proof of your name change and will be required by various institutions when updating your records.

Action Step: Update Identification Documents

Contact the Social Security Administration to update your name on your Social Security card. Update your driver's license, state ID card, and passport by visiting the respective offices with the necessary documents.

Action Step: Inform Financial Institutions and Legal Records

Notify your bank, credit card companies, mortgage lender, and other financial institutions about your name change. Consult with an attorney to update your legal documents, including your will, trust, power of attorney, and advance health care directive.

STEP 4. Establish a new budget

Activity: Assessing Your Financial Situation

Take time to assess your post-divorce financial situation. Consider your income, alimony or child support payments (if applicable), and any changes in living expenses. Reflect on the impact of these factors on your financial well-being.

Exercise: Setting Financial Goals

Establish both short-term and long-term financial goals. Examples include building an emergency fund, saving for retirement, or paying off debt. Prioritize these goals and incorporate them into your budgeting process.

Reflection questions:

How does disentangling yourself financially from your former spouse make you feel?

What will it mean for you to be the only person handling money matters after divorce?

How can you use this opportunity to learn, grow, or regain control over your financial independence?

Evaluating Those Joint Accounts and Assets

Every couple handles their finances differently. Some keep money matters completely separate. Others have everything together and even split the bills 50-50. And some opt for a combination. There's no right or wrong method that works for everyone. No matter what your past approach was, going forward, it's important to find a comfortable, workable situation that you feel is optimal and nurturing for you.

Reflection questions:

Did you and your spouse have individual accounts, joint accounts, or both?

What are your thoughts about how the finances were handled in your relationship?

How did the individual or joint accounts, and shared assets contribute to your overall financial dynamics during the marriage?

In what ways will your closing joint accounts align, or clash, with your long-term financial goals and aspirations?

Moving Toward Financial Empowerment and Independence

Divorce often involves significant financial changes. Evaluate your current financial situation and identify any lingering challenges from your divorce. This includes assessing your assets, debts, and overall financial stability. Write down three practical steps you can take to regain financial stability and independence.

Reflection questions:

How has your divorce impacted your financial situation, and what challenges are you currently facing?

What specific actions can you take to improve your financial stability and regain control?

How can seeking the guidance of a financial advisor or counselor help you create a long-term financial plan?

Exploring Communication and Collaboration

Reflect on your past communication patterns with your former spouse during the marriage. How did these patterns contribute to the challenges or successes in managing joint finances?

Explore any unresolved issues or lingering emotions related to financial matters. How can you process these emotions and establish healthy boundaries during the disentanglement process?

Practice empathy by putting yourself in your former spouse's shoes. How might their perspective and experiences shape their approach to the financial matters associated with your divorce?

How do you think your ex or soon-to-be ex-spouse is faring financially, emotionally, physically, and otherwise? Write down any areas you think they may be struggling. Also, write down what you can do to improve communication.

_____

_____

_____.

Protecting Your Credit During and After Divorce

Your credit score can take an unexpected hit during and after a divorce. Being aware of and reflecting on potential or current challenges can provide valuable insights on how to protect your financial health moving forward. Take some time now to reflect on the emotional and financial impact of credit challenges during or after your divorce. If you had a bitter breakup, consider the pain, anguish, frustration, and anger that may have arisen from dealing with a vindictive ex-spouse or financial sabotage. Use these reflections to fuel your emotional resilience and find strength in navigating the financial aftermath of your breakup.

Engage in reflective writing to explore your attitude toward credit and financial stability after divorce. How can you redefine your relationship with money and credit in a positive and empowering way? Consider whether you need a step-by-step plan to rebuild your credit history, through actions such as monitoring your credit report, making timely payments, and seeking professional advice. How can you stay motivated and accountable throughout this process?

Reflection questions:

Did your ex-spouse do anything—intentional or inadvertent—that hurt your credit or impacted your financial security? If so, what was it and how did you respond to it?

Describe any power and control issues over credit and finances in your marriage. Be honest!

_____

_____

_____.

Exercise: Taking Control of Credit Protection

Consider the actions you can take to protect your credit and regain control of your financial situation. Fill in the blanks with your responses or reflections.

Despite any emotional turmoil of my divorce, I am committed to the following:

To safeguard my credit, I will: _____

_____.

When faced with vindictive actions or financial sabotage, my strategy will be: _____

_____.

The boundaries I will establish to protect my credit include: _____

_____.

Reflecting on my emotional strength, I believe I can overcome financial challenges because: _____

_____.

Creating boundaries and safeguards can go a long way toward protecting your credit and your overall financial health. So think about and develop strategies to establish boundaries and guardrails that would minimize potential conflicts or problems. Fill in the lines with your personalized responses.

In order to protect my credit, I will set clear boundaries by: _____
_____.

To safeguard against potential financial sabotage, I will: _____
_____.

When faced with disputes over joint bills, I will take the following steps to
    ensure my financial stability: _____
_____.

One practical action I can take to maintain control of my credit is:
_____.

    List three qualities or strengths that have helped you navigate the emotional and financial challenges of your divorce:

a. _____

b. _____

c. _____

    How can you leverage these strengths to stay focused and maintain
your financial well-being during this difficult time?

    Reflecting on your resilience, describe one instance where you demonstrated emotional strength in the face of financial adversity caused by your ex-spouse or someone else:
_____
_____.

    By engaging in these activities and exercises, you are not only protecting your credit but also nurturing your emotional resilience. Use the insights gained from reflecting on the drama and challenges to guide your actions and strengthen your determination to overcome financial obstacles. Remember, you have the power to rebuild your credit and create a more secure financial future for yourself.

Creating a Holistic Post-divorce Financial Plan

Divorce necessitates a reassessment of your financial goals and plans. Engage in self-reflection to identify your values, priorities, and aspirations in various areas of life, including finances, relationships, and personal growth. Use creative tools such as vision boards, mind maps, or collages to visualize your desired financial future. Engage in financial self-education through books, podcasts, or workshops to expand your knowledge and confidence in managing your finances independently.

Activity: Creating a Financial Vision Board

Gather magazines, images, and quotes that represent your desired financial future and post-divorce goals. Create a vision board by arranging these elements in a way that resonates with you. Reflect on the images and words you selected for your vision board. What do they represent? How do they inspire and motivate you to take positive financial actions and shape your post-divorce life? Display your vision board in a prominent place where you can see it daily. Use it as a reminder of your financial aspirations and a source of inspiration during challenging moments.

Redefining Personal and Financial Success

Reflect on your previous definitions of personal and financial success within the context of your marriage. How have these definitions evolved since the divorce? How can you redefine success on your own terms?

Consider your values and priorities as you move forward. How can you align your financial decisions and goals with what truly matters to you in life?

Now imagine your ideal post-divorce life. How does it look and feel? How can you take intentional steps to create a life that aligns with your vision of happiness and fulfillment?

Remember, the process of emotional recovery and rebuilding after divorce takes time. Be patient with yourself and allow space for healing, growth, and transformation. Use this *Workbook* as a guide to explore your emotions, gain clarity, and build a stronger foundation for your financial and personal well-being.

You should also take breaks when needed, seek professional guidance if necessary, and celebrate each step forward in your journey of post-divorce healing and empowerment.

Reevaluate Your Insurance Needs

After you separate from a spouse, it's important to examine the insurance policies you had in force and to evaluate your new coverage needs. Take a look at your health, auto, insurance, life, and homeowners/renters insurance plans. See what you need or no longer need and change any beneficiaries as necessary.

Exercise: Health Insurance Assessment

If you were previously covered under your spouse's health insurance plan, explore options to obtain your own coverage. Assess your health care needs and budget to determine the most suitable insurance plan for you. Research options through your employer, the Health Insurance Marketplace, or private insurers.

Exercise: Auto Insurance Review

Update your auto insurance policy to remove your former spouse and adjust coverage levels as needed. Consider changes in names insured, listed drivers, and coverage amounts for liability and comprehensive coverage. Ensure that your policy adequately reflects your current circumstances.

Exercise: Home Insurance Evaluation

If you have moved to a new home or remained in the marital home, review and update your home insurance policy accordingly. Assess changes in ownership, coverage needs, and mortgage information. Adjust policy limits, add or remove coverage endorsements, and obtain coverage for new assets or possessions.

Life Insurance Reassessment

Reassess your life insurance needs in light of your new financial situation. Review the policy's face value, beneficiaries, and premium payments. Consider whether additional coverage is necessary to protect alimony or child support payments in the event of your death.

Reflection questions:

What are your primary concerns or considerations when evaluating your insurance coverage?

How can adequate insurance coverage provide peace of mind and financial protection for you and your loved ones?

By actively engaging in these steps, you are taking proactive measures to regain control over your finances and protect yourself and your loved ones. Embrace the opportunity to establish a solid financial foundation for your future after divorce.

Establishing Long-term Financial Goals

Identifying your long-term financial goals and incorporating them into your divorce proceedings can put you on a path toward long-term financial security.

Exercise questions:

- What is one long-term financial goal that is most important to you?
- What steps can you take to protect your retirement and savings goals during the divorce?
- Do you think seeking the guidance of a financial advisor or counselor can help you create a long-term financial plan? Why or why not?

If you can shift your focus from immediate gains to a more sustainable financial future, prioritizing your needs, but also considering your ex-spouse's needs, you'll typically have a less stressful post-divorce life. So identify your long-term financial goals and develop a plan to incorporate them into your divorce proceedings. Can you recall a specific instance where you prioritized long-term planning over short-term wins during your divorce? How did that decision positively impact your situation? Fill in the blanks with your personalized responses.

One long-term financial goal that is important to me is:

_____.

To prioritize this goal during the divorce process, I will:

_____.

Reflecting on the potential consequences of short-term wins, I am committed to considering the long-term affordability of:

_____.

One step I can take to protect my retirement and savings goals during the divorce is:

_____.

Developing a Cooperative Mindset

Cultivate a cooperative mindset to facilitate long-term planning and minimize future conflicts with your ex-spouse. Fill in the lines with your personalized responses.

Despite any negative emotions, I am committed to:

_____.

To promote cooperation during the divorce process, I will:

_____.

When faced with potential disputes or disagreements, my strategy will be to:

_____.

One practical action I can take to maintain a cooperative mindset is:

_____.

Prioritizing the Well-being of Your Children

Consider the long-term impact of divorce on your children's well-being and incorporate their needs into your planning process.

List three ways in which you can prioritize the well-being of your children during and after the divorce:

a. _____

b. _____

c. _____

How can you ensure that your financial decisions align with the best interests of your children's future?

Reflecting on the importance of your children's financial stability, describe one instance where you made a decision that positively impacted their well-being:

_____.

By engaging in these activities and exercises, you are not only protecting your financial future but also fostering a cooperative mindset and prioritizing the well-being of your children. Use the insights gained from reflecting on the importance of long-term planning and avoiding common financial mistakes to guide your actions and secure a more stable and fulfilling post-divorce life. By making thoughtful and rational decisions, you are paving the way for less animosity and an all-around better future for yourself and your family.

Although divorce can stir a whirlwind of emotions, often prompting hasty decisions, staying focusing on long-term financial stability can ensure a more secure future.

Reflection questions:

- How have impulsive decisions during the divorce process affected your financial well-being and long-term prospects?
- Reflecting on your financial goals, what are the key benefits of prioritizing long-term planning during divorce?

Case Studies: Two Post-divorce Stories of Emotional Recovery

The stories of Pamela Zapata and my sister, Cheryl Brown, offer valuable insights into the process of emotional recovery after divorce. Reread their stories at the end of the divorce chapter in *Bounce Back* and then answer the following questions to boost your own emotional well-being.

Reflection questions:

- How did Pamela's story resonate with your own experiences or fears regarding financial matters during your divorce?
- How has Cheryl's story of transformation challenged or inspired your perception of post-divorce relationships?

- Do you know any couples such as Cheryl and her ex-husband, William, who have divorced and later became friends? What did they do to get there?

Strategies for Your Emotional Recovery

Drawing lessons from Pamela and Cheryl's experiences, let's create your personalized strategy for emotional recovery after divorce.

Exercise questions:

- What key insights have you gained from Pamela's and Cheryl's stories?
- How can you prioritize your children's well-being and establish effective communication and cooperation with your ex-spouse?
- What key takeaways can you apply to foster effective co-parenting and prioritize your children's well-being?
- How can Cheryl's story, of successfully co-parenting and becoming friends with her ex-spouse, empower you to let go of resentment and build a cooperative mindset for the benefit of your family?

Learning from Others

One key insight I gained from Pamela's story is:

_____.

Action step: To prioritize my financial well-being, I will:

_____.

Cheryl's transformation from a contentious divorce to successful co-parenting taught me:

_____.

Action step: To improve my post-divorce relationship, I will:

_____.

Prioritizing the well-being of my children is crucial. I will focus on effective co-parenting by:

_____.

Action step: To support my children's well-being, I will:

_____.

By engaging in these activities and exercises, you are taking active steps toward emotional recovery and creating a positive post-divorce life. Use the insights gained from the activities in this chapter and your reflections—of both your own situation and the stories of Pamela Zapata and Cheryl Brown—to guide your actions and foster a stronger sense of emotional well-being. Remember, you are not alone in surviving a relationship breakup. By prioritizing your emotional health and your finances, you can build a fulfilling and joyful life after divorce.

As we conclude this fourth chapter of *The Bounce Back Workbook*, which focused on divorce, take time to think about what you have just done, felt, and discovered. What emotions surfaced for you during the exercises? What lessons have you learned so far, and what growth have you experienced? Write a recap below.

_____

_____

_____

_____

_____

Chapter 5

Death of a Loved One

Losing a loved one is an incredibly challenging experience that encompasses not only emotional pain but also significant financial and practical challenges. In this chapter, we'll tackle the profound complexities of grief and loss and provide strategies for healing, navigating financial difficulties, and addressing ancillary losses. Through reflection, action, and support, you can find strength and resilience in the face of loss, and begin to rebuild your life with a renewed sense of purpose.

Activity: Reflection and Healing

Reflect on Verlaina Warner Brown's story of losing her husband during the COVID-19 pandemic, and consider how you can cope with the emotional and financial challenges of losing a loved one. Use these reflections to develop strategies for healing and moving forward.

Reflection questions:

How does Verlaina's experience of losing her husband during the pandemic resonate with your own experiences or fears surrounding death and loss?

Reflecting on Verlaina's initial reaction to her husband's death, how have you personally coped with the grief and shock of losing a loved one?

How has the loss of a loved one impacted your financial situation, and what emotions or challenges has it brought up for you?

How have you navigated financial changes and communicated them to your family members or dependents after the loss of a loved one?

What steps can you take to begin healing and rebuilding your life after the death of a loved one?

Exercise: Strategies for Healing and Moving Forward

Develop personalized strategies for coping with grief and rebuilding your life based on the lessons learned from Verlaina Warner Brown's story. Fill in the blanks with your own reflections and action steps.

One key insight I gained from Verlaina's story is:

_____.

Action step: To cope with grief, I will:

_____.

Reflecting on my own emotions and challenges after losing a loved one, I recognize the importance of seeking support. One support system I will reach out to is:

_____.

Action step: To nurture my emotional well-being, I will:

_____.

Verlaina faced financial adjustments after the loss of her spouse. In order to address my financial challenges, I will:

_____.

Action step: To manage my finances effectively, I will:

_____.

Verlaina had to communicate financial limitations to her children. To navigate similar conversations with my family members, I will:

_____.

Action step: To foster understanding and support, I will:

_____.

Verlaina's journey toward emotional and financial recovery inspires me to take steps toward rebuilding my life. One action I will take to begin the healing process is:

_____.

Action step: To move forward and rebuild, I will:

_____.

By engaging in these activities and exercises, you are taking active measures to progress in the direction of healing and moving forward after the death of a loved one. Use the insights gained from reflecting on Verlaina Warner Brown's story to guide your actions and foster emotional and financial well-being. Remember to be patient and kind to yourself as you navigate the process of healing and rebuilding your life.

Navigating Financial Grief and Rebuilding

Losing a loved one brings not only emotional pain but also significant financial challenges. Recall the major drop in income Verlaina experienced, and consider your circumstances. They may be similar or very different. Whatever the case, use the following reflections to develop strategies for coping and moving forward.

Reflection questions:

How have you coped with grief and managed the financial impact of losing a loved one in your own life?

Have you considered seeking professional support to help navigate your grief and financial challenges?

What personal belongings of your deceased loved one did you have difficulty parting with and why?

What activities did you formerly do with your loved one that you no longer do?

Are there some things you still do, perhaps to keep alive the memory of the person who passed?

Exercise: Strategies for Coping and Rebuilding

Develop personalized strategies for coping with grief and rebuilding your life based on the lessons learned from Verlaina Warner Brown's story. Fill in the blanks with your own reflections and action steps.

One key insight I gained from Verlaina's story is:

_____.

Action step: To cope with grief, I will:

_____.

Reflecting on my own emotions and financial challenges after losing a loved one, I recognize the importance of seeking professional support. One professional resource I will reach out to is:

_____.

Action step: To navigate my grief effectively, I will:

_____.

Verlaina faced the difficult task of letting go of her deceased spouse's belongings and adjusting daily habits. To address similar challenges, I will:

_____.

Action step: To create space for healing, I will:

_____.

Verlaina emphasized the importance of physical health and addressing financial responsibilities. To take care of myself physically and financially, I will:

_____.

Action step: To prioritize my well-being, I will:

_____.

Verlaina's journey toward rebuilding her life inspires me to take steps toward my own recovery. One action I will take to begin to bounce back is:

_____.

Action step: To move forward and rebuild, I will:

Reflections

Do you feel guilty if you laugh or experience any happiness? If so, why?

Do you feel like everyone has moved on and forgotten about you, your grief, or the person who passed? If so, why?

By engaging in these activities and exercises, you are taking active steps toward coping with grief and rebuilding your life after the death of a loved one. Use the insights gained from reflecting on Verlaina Warner Brown's story to guide your actions and foster emotional and financial well-being. Remember to be patient and kind to yourself as you navigate the process of healing and rebuilding your life.

Understanding and Addressing Ancillary Losses

Losing a loved one brings not only the primary loss of the person but also ancillary losses that can compound grief and affect your overall well-being. Take a moment to acknowledge the ancillary losses you have experienced or are currently facing after the death of your loved one. Reflect on how these losses have impacted different aspects of your life.

Ancillary losses reflection:

Emotional support: How has the absence of your loved one affected the emotional support you used to receive? In what ways has this loss left you feeling isolated or overwhelmed?

Financial stability: Has the death of a breadwinner or financial contributor caused a significant decline in your financial situation? How has this loss impacted your lifestyle or living conditions?

Roles and responsibilities: What roles and responsibilities did your loved one fulfill that you or other family members now need to take on? How has this adjustment added stress or caused identity shifts?

Social connections: Did the deceased play a central role in your social circle? How has their absence affected your relationships with friends, neighbors, and extended family?

Shared dreams and plans: What dreams and plans did you have with the deceased for the future? How has the loss of these anticipated experiences affected you?

Sense of self: Did your identity or sense of self rely on your relationship with the deceased? How has their passing impacted your perception of yourself?

Familiar routines: How have daily routines and rituals that involved the deceased been disrupted? How has this loss of structure affected your life?

Exercise: Addressing Ancillary Losses

Now that you have acknowledged your ancillary losses, it's important to address them to facilitate healing and support your recovery. Consider the following strategies to help navigate these secondary losses and their impact on your life.

Seek emotional support: Connect with friends, family, or a support group to help fill the void of emotional support left by your loved one's absence. Sharing your feelings and experiences with others who understand can provide comfort and a sense of community.

Financial planning and support: If the loss has affected your financial stability, consider seeking financial advice or working with a financial planner to navigate the challenges and develop a plan for the future. Explore potential sources of financial support, such as life insurance, government benefits, or community resources.

Redefine your roles and responsibilities: As you adjust to the new circumstances, reassess roles and responsibilities within your family or support network. Delegate tasks or seek assistance when needed to alleviate stress and prevent feeling overwhelmed. Remember that it's OK to ask for help.

Nurture social connections: Invest in maintaining and building new social connections. Reach out to friends, reconnect with supportive family members, or consider joining community groups or organizations that align with your interests. Engaging in social activities can provide companionship and a sense of belonging.

Adapt your dreams and plans: While it may be difficult to let go of shared dreams and plans, take time to reflect and adjust your expectations. Explore new possibilities and set new goals that align with your current circumstances. Allow yourself to embrace new opportunities and experiences.

Rediscover your sense of self: Take the time to explore and redefine your sense of self. Reflect on your personal values, interests, and strengths. Engage in activities that bring you joy and allow you to express yourself. Embracing your identity and nurturing your own growth can help you navigate the process of redefining yourself without the presence of your loved one.

Establish new routines and rituals: Create new daily routines and rituals that provide structure and stability in your life. This can help fill the void left by disrupted routines and provide a sense of comfort and normalcy.

Practice self-care: Prioritize self-care to support your physical and emotional well-being. This includes maintaining a healthy lifestyle through proper nutrition, regular exercise, and sufficient rest. Engage in activities that bring you peace and relaxation, such as meditation, yoga, or spending time in nature.

Seek professional help: If you find it challenging to cope with the ancillary losses and navigate the grieving process on your own, consider seeking professional help. Grief counseling, therapy, or support from a qualified mental health professional can provide valuable guidance, tools, and encouragement tailored to your specific needs.

Practice patience and self-compassion: Remember that healing takes time, and everyone's journey is unique. Be patient with yourself as you navigate the complex emotions and challenges that come with grief and loss. Practice self-compassion and allow yourself to grieve in your own way and at your own pace. Processing the death of a loved one is a transition that often takes years. So don't rush and don't judge yourself if you have bouts of crying or feelings of deep loss or regret.

Addressing ancillary losses is an ongoing process that may require revisiting and adapting strategies as you continue to heal and grow. Give yourself permission to grieve, seek support when needed, and embrace the resilience within you as you navigate the path to recovery.

In the next sections, we will explore additional aspects of coping with the death of a loved one, including finding meaning in the midst of grief. We'll also look at your finances and what you can do to shore up yourself economically.

The Six Transition Truths

In *Bounce Back*, I shared the Six Transition Truths as put forth by the Sudden Money Institute. Reread those now if you need an explainer because these truths are not only vitally important but also extremely helpful to keep in mind as you process the reality of losing a loved one. This processing obviously doesn't happen overnight, or even for weeks and months. It takes years. To better understand and personalize the concepts behind these transition truths, complete the following worksheet, and refer back to it often.

Worksheet: Navigating Transition Truths

Transition Truth No. 1: Resist the Urge to DO

Exercise: Reflecting on Action vs. Nonaction

Financial planners, grief counselors, and others say you should avoid making any important decisions or jumping into activities as a way to avoid dealing with the emotional fallout of losing a loved one. Take some time to reflect on the concept of resisting the urge to take immediate action during a major life transition. Answer the following questions:

What tasks or decisions have you felt pressured to perform or make since experiencing your loss?

How did (or do) you feel during those moments of pressure? Did you feel calm and clear-headed, or overwhelmed and confused?

Are there any specific tasks or decisions that you rushed into and now regret?

How do you think your transition experience might have been different if you had taken more time and resisted the urge to rush into action?

_____

_____

_____

_____

Transition Truth No. 2: You Have a Say in the Matter

Exercise: Examining Your Narratives

Explore the narratives you have created about your life and the stories you've been telling yourself about the events surrounding your loss. Consider the following prompts:

Reflect on the narratives you have developed about your relationships, future, and your perspective on money since the loss. Are these narratives serving you well or contributing to feeling overwhelmed and negative?

Identify any recurring negative thoughts or internal dialogues that arise. Write them down and challenge their validity. Are these thoughts based on evidence or assumptions?

Consider how you can cultivate more compassionate and empowering narratives. What changes can you make to create a more positive and supportive internal dialogue?

Explore alternative perspectives and outcomes. How might the story of your life unfold differently from what you initially envisioned? What new possibilities might arise?

_____

_____

_____

_____

Transition Truths 3–6: Altering Identity, Letting Go, Defining What's Important, and New Possibilities

Exercise: Exploring Personal Transformation

Reflect on these transition truths and how they apply to your own experience. Use the following prompts to guide your reflections:

Identity: How has your sense of self and identity shifted since the loss? What aspects of your identity have been altered, and what new aspects are emerging?

Letting go: What attachments or expectations have you had to release during this transition? How have you coped with the process of letting go?

What's important: Identify the aspects of your life that hold vital importance to you. What values, relationships, or principles do you want to protect and prioritize during this transition? How can you ensure they are honored?

(Continued)

New possibilities: Explore the potential for new opportunities and possibilities that may arise from this transition. What positive changes or experiences do you envision for your future?

_____

_____

_____

_____

Reflection: Finding Meaning and Moving Forward

Reflect on the Six Transition Truths and how they can guide you toward finding meaning and moving forward in the face of loss. Write a personal reflection addressing the following points:

How have these transition truths helped you reframe your perspective on your current situation?

What new insights or realizations have you gained from contemplating these truths?

How can you use these transition truths to discover meaning, find new purpose, and move forward in your journey of healing and rebuilding?

What steps or actions can you take to embrace these transition truths and apply them to your life moving forward?

_____

_____

_____

_____

Remember to revisit these reflections and exercises whenever you feel overwhelmed or uncertain during your transition. They serve as reminders of your agency and ability to navigate the challenges and embrace the possibilities that lie ahead.

Taking the First Crucial Five Steps

Step 1: Give Yourself Time to Grieve

Reflection:

Take some time to reflect on your grieving process and prioritize your emotional well-being. Answer the following questions:

How have you been allowing yourself to grieve since the loss of your loved one?

Have you experienced any pressures or expectations to move on or take immediate action? How have these external influences affected your grieving process?

Action steps:

✓ Identify specific self-care practices that support your emotional well-being, such as journaling, meditation, spending time in nature, or engaging in creative outlets.

✓ Reach out to friends, family, or support groups to share your feelings and seek comfort.

✓ Give yourself permission to feel and express your emotions without judgment or pressure to move on quickly. Everyone processes grief in their own time and way.

Step 2: Locate and Organize Important Documents

Reflection:

When you're emotionally ready to tend to financial matters or legal paperwork, begin the process of locating and organizing important documents. Answer the following questions:

How do you feel tending to financial and legal matters?

What support, if any, do you need to handle the task of finding and organizing important documents after your loved one's passing?

What concerns or challenges do you anticipate in this process?

How do you think having organized documents will benefit you during the financial recovery process?

Action steps:
- ✓ Start by identifying specific places where important documents might be located, such as filing cabinets, safes, or digital storage.
- ✓ Create a checklist of the essential documents to locate, including wills, insurance policies, and financial statements.
- ✓ Develop a system for organizing and storing these documents, whether physically or digitally, to ensure easy access when needed.

Step 3: Inform Relevant Parties and Institutions

Reflection:

Consider the importance of notifying relevant parties and institutions about your loved one's passing. Answer the following questions:

How do you feel about the process of notifying organizations about the death of your loved one?

Would you rather assign this task to someone else? Why or why not?

Are there any specific concerns or uncertainties you have regarding these notifications?

How do you think completing this step will contribute to your financial recovery and protect against potential issues?

Action steps:
- ✓ Obtain multiple certified copies of the death certificate to provide as proof when notifying organizations.
- ✓ Create a list of organizations to contact, prioritizing those with the most significant impact on your financial situation or legal responsibilities.
- ✓ Keep track of your communications, including dates, names of representatives, and relevant reference numbers.
- ✓ Seek assistance from professionals, such as attorneys or financial advisors, if you encounter complications or have questions during the notification process.

Step 4: Assess Your Financial Situation

Reflection:

Reflect on how financially stable or potentially precarious you may feel. Answer the following questions:

How do you feel about taking stock of your loved one's assets, debts, and ongoing expenses?

What concerns or uncertainties do you have regarding this assessment?

How do you think understanding your financial situation will impact your ability to make informed decisions and plan for the future?

Action steps:
- ✓ Create an inventory of your loved one's assets, including bank accounts, investment accounts, real estate, and vehicles.
- ✓ Identify debts and ongoing expenses, such as credit card balances, loans, mortgages, and utility bills.
- ✓ Determine sources of income and financial support, such as insurance payouts, Social Security benefits, and inheritances.
- ✓ Consult with professionals, such as financial advisors or estate attorneys, to ensure a thorough assessment of your financial situation.

Step 5: Create a New Budget and Financial Plan

Reflection:

To what extent will your loved one's death affect your personal budget? Answer the following questions:

How do you feel about creating a new budget and adjusting your financial goals?

Are there any fears or challenges you anticipate in this process?

Action steps:
- ✓ Determine your new sources of income and ongoing expenses.
- ✓ Create a detailed budget that prioritizes essential expenses and allows for discretionary spending.
- ✓ Make necessary adjustments to accommodate your new financial situation, such as cutting back on nonessential expenses or finding additional sources of income.
- ✓ Consider building an emergency fund to provide a financial cushion for unexpected expenses.
- ✓ Reevaluate your financial goals and adjust savings and investment strategies accordingly.
- ✓ Seek professional guidance to develop a customized budget and financial plan that considers your unique circumstances and goals.

By completing these worksheets and action steps, you will be well on your way to taking the crucial first steps toward financial recovery and stability after the loss of a loved one. Remember to be patient with yourself and seek support from professionals and loved ones as needed throughout the process.

As we conclude this fifth chapter of *The Bounce Back Workbook*, which focused on the death of a loved one, take time to think about what you have just done, felt, and discovered. What emotions surfaced for you during the exercises? What lessons have you learned so far, and what growth have you experienced? Write a recap below.

_____

_____

_____

_____

_____

Chapter 6

Disability

Living with a disability creates challenges—as well as opportunities for growth and development. In this chapter of *The Bounce Back Workbook*, we'll examine the emotional, physical, and financial realities facing disabled people and their caregivers. Whether you have a disability or are supporting someone who does, the exercises that follow are designed to empower you to overcome obstacles, embrace your capabilities, and find financial stability and personal fulfillment. Even if you are a caregiver, I encourage you to complete the activities and reflections from your own perspective.

No matter what your circumstances, living with a disability does not define you. It is one aspect of who you are. By harnessing your unique strengths and seeking the support and resources available to you, you can create a life that is rich in experiences, personal growth, and economic well-being. Ultimately, I hope the information within these pages will help you not only to better cope with a disability but also gain a deeper sense of control and contentment in your life.

Activity: Reflection on Personal Experience with Disabilities

Take a moment to reflect on your own personal experience with disabilities. Whether you have a disability yourself, care for someone with a disability, or have encountered disabilities in your community, consider the following questions:

Have you or someone close to you ever experienced a disability? If so, what was the nature of the disability, and how did it impact your life, or the life of the individual affected?

_____

_____

_____

_____.

How long have you (or someone close to you) had the disability? Has it been all your life or in recent months or years?

_____

_____

_____.

How did you (or someone close to you) initially react to the disability?

_____

_____

_____.

How have other people reacted to your (or your relative's/friend's) disability?

_____

_____

_____.

What emotions or thoughts arise when you think about your (or your relative's/friend's) disability?

_____

_____

_____.

Reflecting on your experience, what positive aspects or personal growth
have you witnessed as a result of encountering a disability or supporting a loved one? Did it change your perspective or provide new insights?

_____

_____

_____

_____.

What resources or support systems have you used to navigate any challenges associated with the disability? How did these resources assist
you in coping or adapting to the situation?

_____

_____

_____

_____.

Remember, there are no right or wrong answers, and this activity is meant
to encourage self-reflection and exploration.

Other thoughts and reflections:

1. _____.

2. _____.

3. _____.

Activity: Assessing Your Disability Insurance Needs

Assessing your disability insurance needs is an important step in protecting
your financial well-being in the event of a disability. Consider the following
questions to evaluate your current situation and determine the level of disability insurance coverage that may be appropriate for you:

Do you currently have disability insurance coverage? If yes, what type of coverage do you have (short-term or long-term)? If no, why have you not
obtained disability insurance coverage?

Are you familiar with the disability insurance options offered by your employer? If yes, what are the coverage details, and how does it align with your needs? If not, consider reaching out to your employer's human resources department to gather information about disability insurance options available to you.

Evaluating Your Financial Picture

Assess your financial obligations and determine the minimum amount of income replacement you would need in the event of a disability. Consider your monthly expenses, including housing costs, utility bills, groceries, medical expenses, debt payments, and other financial obligations.

Evaluate your current savings and emergency fund too. How many months of living expenses could you cover with your savings alone? Consider whether this would be sufficient to sustain you in the event of a disability.

Reflect on your current health condition and the potential risks associated with your occupation or lifestyle. Are you at a higher risk for a disability due to your work environment, health history, or other factors?

Three Disability Insurance Action Steps

1. Make a list of questions that you have about disability insurance.

_____

_____

_____

_____.

2. Research the disability insurance options available to you outside of your employer-sponsored coverage.
3. Consider private disability insurance policies that may offer more comprehensive coverage or supplement your existing coverage.
4. Consult with a financial advisor or insurance professional to understand the specific terms, coverage limits, waiting periods, and exclusions associated with disability insurance policies. They can answer questions, help you assess your needs, and provide guidance on the best options available to you.

Take the time to get answers to your questions and gather the necessary information to make informed decisions about disability insurance coverage. It's important to protect yourself and your financial well-being in the event of a disability. Remember, this activity is meant to guide your assessment, and seeking professional advice is recommended to ensure you have the appropriate coverage for your unique situation.

Reflections or information learned:

1. _____.

2. _____.

3. _____.

Navigating Disability Benefits

Let's now explore the topics of Social Security Disability Insurance (SSDI) and Workers' Compensation. These exercises and reflections that follow are designed to help you deepen your understanding of these areas and consider their financial and emotional implications. Take your time to complete each step and feel free to write your answers and thoughts in this *Workbook*.

Reflection questions:

In 2023, the maximum SSDI payment amount was $3,627, and the average payment was $1,358. Experts expect payments in 2024 to increase by 3.1%. (Payments are tied to inflation, so they adjust annually.)

How would receiving SSDI benefits impact your current financial situation?

_____

_____.

What specific financial challenges would SSDI benefits help you address?

_____

_____.

Are there any financial concerns or uncertainties that arise when considering SSDI benefits?

_____

_____.

How would receiving SSDI benefits affect your emotional well-being?

_____

_____.

Are there any emotional barriers or fears you associate with applying for SSDI benefits?

_____

_____.

What emotional support or coping strategies might you need while navigating the SSDI application process?

_____

_____.

The Social Security Administration bases your SSDI payment amount on your average covered earnings over several years. SSA uses a formula to arrive at a figure called your PIA—your primary insurance amount—which is how much you'll receive each month. To find out what your PIA is, you have a few options:

- Call your local SSA office;
- Call the National SSA number at 1-800-772-1213;
- Use SSA's online benefits calculator (it's online at ssa.gov); or
- Create a myssa.com account.

Exploring Workers' Compensation

You may recall from the main *Bounce Back* book that Workers' Compensation provides financial benefits in the event of a work-related injury or illness. This economic support can help you cover medical expenses and maintain your standard of living. But sometimes people don't apply for the benefits for which they're eligible mainly because the task seems too difficult. Consider your capacity to press forward and collect on payouts that may be due to you.

Reflection questions:

Are there any financial considerations or limitations associated with Workers' Compensation that concern you?

_____

_____.

How might the process of filing a Workers' Compensation claim impact your emotional well-being?

_____

_____.

Are there any emotional concerns or anxieties that arise when thinking about relying on Workers' Compensation benefits?

_____

_____.

What emotional support systems or resources might be helpful to you throughout the Workers' Compensation process?

_____

_____.

Remember, these reflections and exercises are intended to support your personal exploration and understanding of SSDI and Workers' Compensation. Take the time to delve into your thoughts and feelings, and use this *Workbook* as a tool to gain clarity and insight. If you feel overwhelmed or uncertain at any point, consider seeking guidance from professionals or support networks specializing in disability benefits and legal matters.

Recognizing the Emotional Journey

Coping with a disability also involves navigating a complex emotional landscape. It is important to acknowledge and address these emotions to promote healing and resilience. Consider the following questions to explore your emotional journey:

How has your disability, or that of your loved one, affected your emotional well-being and sense of identity?

_____

_____

_____ .

What strategies or coping mechanisms have you found helpful in managing emotional challenges?

_____

_____

_____ .

Are there any negative or limiting beliefs about your or your loved one's disability that you would like to challenge?

_____

_____

_____ .

How can you cultivate a positive mindset and maintain emotional balance throughout your journey?

_____

_____

_____ .

Looking Inward as a Caregiver

Caring for others often means neglecting yourself. Reflect on how this shows up in your life, and write down your answers to the following questions:

When did you last do something purely for your own enjoyment? What gets in the way of making time for yourself?

_____

_____

_____

Do you minimize your own needs and emotions in order to prioritize the person you care for? How might suppressing your feelings impact you?

_____

_____

_____

In what ways has your health (physical, mental, emotional, or financial) been compromised by the demands of caregiving? What small steps could you take to improve your well-being?

_____

_____

_____

Is your self-worth tied to being a caregiver? Where do you think these beliefs originated? How else can you find meaning and purpose?

_____

_____

_____

If caregiving ended tomorrow, who would you be? What parts of yourself have been lost in your role? How can you reconnect with your core identity outside of caregiving?

_____

_____

_____

What support do you need but aren't receiving? What is holding you back from asking for help? How could you build a community that cares for both you and your loved one?

_____

_____

_____

Take some time with these reflections. Your needs matter too. Prioritizing your own well-being will ultimately allow you to be fully present as a caregiver. You are worthy of care.

Activity: Exploring Alternative Income Sources

TEST YOUR KNOWLEDGE

Do you recall the six types of income mentioned in Bounce Back that disabled people can access? If so write as many as you remember on the lines below.

1. Income source: _____

2. Income source: _____

3. Income source: _____

4. Income source: _____

5. Income source: _____

6. Income source: _____

Don't worry if you couldn't recall everything! Let's now drill down deeper into the six alternative income sources for individuals with disabilities. Take your time to evaluate the feasibility of each source and consider the financial and emotional aspects associated with them. Feel free to write your answers and thoughts in this *Workbook* as you assess each financial source.

Income Source 1: Government Benefits

Financial reflections:

Do you have any reservations about getting government benefits? Why or why not?

_____

_____.

How would receiving government benefits, such as SSDI or SSI, impact your financial stability?

_____

_____.

What are the potential benefits and limitations of relying on government assistance for income?

_____

_____.

Are there any financial concerns or uncertainties that arise when considering government benefits?

_____

_____.

Are there any emotional barriers or fears associated with applying for or receiving government benefits?

_____

_____.

What emotional support or coping strategies might be helpful while navigating government benefit programs?

_____

_____.

Income Source 2: Disability Insurance

Financial reflections:

How would you manage economically during the interim waiting period before disability coverage takes effect?

Taking your condition into account, what type of disability insurance policies would make the most sense: short- or long-term coverage? And why?

Income Source 3: Personal Savings and Investments

Financial reflections:

How would relying on personal savings and investments provide financial stability during a period of disability?

_____

_____.

What are the potential benefits and risks of using personal savings and investments as an income source?

_____

_____

_____.

Describe any financial considerations or uncertainties associated with relying on personal savings and investments.

_____

_____

_____.

How realistic is it for you to live off your savings or investments, and how
   long would your money last?

_____

_____

_____.

Income Source 4: Passive Income

Financial reflections:

How would generating passive income contribute to your financial stability
   during a period of disability?

_____

_____

_____.

What are the potential benefits and challenges of pursuing passive
   income streams?

_____

_____

_____.

Are there any financial considerations or limitations associated with generating passive income?

_____

_____

_____.

How might pursuing or building up your passive income base impact your
   emotional or financial well-being?

_____

_____

_____.

Are there any emotional challenges or worries that arise when considering passive income options?

_____

_____

_____.

What emotional resources or self-care practices might be beneficial in managing the emotional aspects of generating passive income?

_____

_____

_____.

Income Source 5: Support from Family and Friends

Financial reflections:

How would receiving financial support from family and friends impact your financial situation during a period of disability?

_____

_____

_____.

What are the potential benefits and limitations of relying on support from loved ones for income?

_____

_____

_____.

What are the practical financial considerations or concerns that you have associated with receiving support from family and friends?

_____

_____

_____.

How might relying on support from family and friends for income affect
your well-being and relationships?

_____

_____

_____.

Income Source 6: Reverse Mortgages

Financial reflections:

Given the age and financial requirements (you must be 62 and have a lot of
equity in your home), how practical and feasible is it for you to consider
a reverse mortgage?

_____

_____.

How would getting a reverse mortgage impact your financial stability?

_____

_____.

What do you think the pros and cons are of utilizing a reverse mortgage as
an income source?

_____

_____

_____.

What financial concerns, questions, or uncertainties do you have about
reverse mortgages?

_____

_____

_____.

How might utilizing a reverse mortgage impact your emotional well-being and sense of independence?

_____

_____.

Are there any emotional challenges or worries that arise when considering reverse mortgages?

_____

_____

_____.

Remember, these reflections and exercises are intended to support your personal exploration and understanding of alternative income sources when you have a disability. Take the time to delve into your thoughts and feelings, and use this workbook as a tool to gain clarity and insight. If you feel overwhelmed or uncertain at any point, consider seeking guidance from professionals or support networks specializing in disability benefits and financial planning.

Support Systems and Coping Strategies

Building a strong support system and employing effective coping strategies are vital in navigating the physical and emotional aspects of disability. Consider the following areas of support and coping mechanisms.

Activity: Acknowledging a Personal Strength

Reflection: Reflect on a recent accomplishment or personal strength that you are proud of. Write about how this achievement has impacted your mindset and attitude toward your disability, or your role as a caregiver.

_____

_____

_____

The exercise above can help you shift your focus toward the aspects of your life where you have abilities, and strengths—as opposed to only being preoccupied with something you can't do.

Engaging in Regular Physical Activity

To boost your emotional well-being and physical resilience too, consult with your health care team and develop an exercise plan tailored to your abilities. Start by incorporating gentle stretches or low-impact exercises into your routine. Keep track of your progress and any improvements you notice over time.

Reflections:
Write about how engaging in physical activity—at whatever level you have
   capacity—has impacted your overall well-being. How does it make you
   feel physically, emotionally, and mentally? Are there any challenges
   you've encountered, and how have you overcome them?

_____

_____

_____.

Seeking Social Support

Reach out to a support group or online community related to your specific disability or condition. Introduce yourself, share your story, and engage in conversations with others who can relate to your experiences. By being connected to others, you'll better manage your disability and the physical or emotional challenges you may face.

Reflection:
Reflect on a meaningful connection or support you have received from
   someone within your support network. Describe how this interaction
   has made a difference in your life and provided a sense of comfort or
   understanding.

_____

_____

_____.

Utilize Therapy and Counseling

Schedule a session with a therapist or counselor to discuss your experiences, emotions, and challenges related to your disability. Take note of any strategies or coping mechanisms they suggest during your session.

Reflection:
Write about a significant insight or breakthrough you have had during therapy or counseling sessions. How has it influenced your perception of your disability and your ability to cope with its impact on your life?

_____

_____

_____.

Consider Complementary and Alternative Therapies

Research and explore a complementary therapy that interests you, such as acupuncture, massage, or yoga. Schedule a consultation or try a beginner's class to experience the potential benefits.

Reflection:
Reflect on your experience with a complementary therapy you have tried or researched. How did it make you feel physically and emotionally? Did it have any positive effects on managing your disability-related symptoms?

_____

_____

_____.

Foster a Sense of Purpose

Explore different hobbies or volunteer opportunities that align with your interests and values. Engage in at least one activity that brings you a sense of purpose or fulfillment each week.

Reflection:

Write about a recent experience or accomplishment related to your chosen hobby or volunteer work. How has it contributed to your overall well-being and sense of purpose? Describe any positive effects it has had on your mindset and outlook on life.

_____

_____

_____.

Remember, these activities, exercises, and reflections are meant to be personalized and adapted to your specific situation and abilities. Take your time, be patient with yourself, and celebrate small victories along the way. If you find it challenging to complete any of these exercises independently, consider involving a trusted friend, family member, or health care professional who can provide support and guidance throughout the process.

Reflections on personal support:

Who are the individuals in your life who can provide emotional support during challenging times?

How can you communicate your needs to your loved ones and involve them in your journey?

Are there support groups or communities where you can connect with others facing similar challenges?

Reflections on physical support:

What health care professionals or specialists can assist you in managing your disability and improving your physical well-being?

Have you explored adaptive technologies, mobility aids, or home modifications that can enhance your independence and daily life activities?

How can regular physical activity, adapted to your abilities, contribute to your overall well-being?

Reflections on financial support:

Have you thoroughly explored disability insurance options, such as short-term and long-term disability coverage? If not, what is holding you back?

Are you aware of your eligibility status for government programs, such as Social Security Disability Insurance, that can provide financial support in case of disability?

Have you considered consulting with financial advisors or experts who can guide you in managing your finances effectively? Why or why not?

_____

_____

_____.

Exploring Adaptive Strategies

Adaptive strategies play a crucial role in empowering people with disabilities to lead fulfilling lives. These strategies include assistive technology, home modifications, adaptive clothing, and participation in adaptive sports and recreational activities. You may not have considered all of the ways that adaptive strategies can be transformational in your life. So here's a checklist of ways to incorporate various strategies and tools into your everyday activities.

Adaptive Strategies Checklist: 10 Ways You Can Use Adaptive Strategies

1. _____**Assistive technology:** Utilize various assistive technologies designed to help individuals with disabilities complete daily tasks more easily. Examples include voice recognition software for those with limited hand mobility, screen readers for individuals with visual impairments, and hearing aids for those with hearing loss.
2. _____**Home modifications:** Adapt your living environment to accommodate your specific needs. This can involve installing ramps for wheelchair access, widening doorways, adding grab bars in bathrooms, or modifying countertops and cabinets for easier access.
3. _____**Mobility aids:** Use mobility aids, such as wheelchairs, walkers, or canes, to help you move around more easily and independently. These aids can help you conserve energy, reduce pain, and improve your overall mobility.
4. _____**Task simplification:** Break down complex tasks into smaller, more manageable steps. This can help you accomplish daily activities more easily and with less frustration. For example, if preparing a meal is challenging, consider using pre-chopped ingredients or utilizing adaptive kitchen tools, such as one-handed can openers or utensil grips.

5. _____**Energy conservation techniques:** Learn to prioritize and pace your activities to conserve energy and prevent fatigue. This can involve scheduling rest breaks, alternating between high- and low-energy tasks, or delegating certain tasks to others when possible.

6. _____**Adaptive clothing:** Choose clothing that is easy to put on and take off, such as garments with Velcro closures, magnetic fasteners, or elastic waistbands. This can help you maintain your independence and reduce the time and effort required to dress and undress.

7. _____**Adaptive hobbies and sports:** Find ways to continue participating in hobbies or sports that you enjoy, even with your physical limitations. Many adaptive sports organizations and recreational programs offer modified versions of popular activities, such as wheelchair basketball, adaptive skiing, or seated yoga.

8. _____**Communication strategies:** If your disability affects your ability to communicate, explore alternative communication methods. This can include using communication boards, sign language, or augmentative and alternative communication (AAC) devices.

9. _____**Transportation adaptations:** If your disability affects your ability to drive, consider adapting your vehicle with hand controls, wheelchair lifts, or other modifications that can help you maintain your independence and mobility. Alternatively, explore public transportation options or paratransit services that accommodate individuals with disabilities.

10. _____**Professional support services:** Seek the assistance of professionals who specialize in working with individuals with disabilities. These services can include occupational therapy, physical therapy, speech therapy, and vocational rehabilitation. These professionals can help you develop personalized strategies and techniques to overcome specific challenges related to your disability, enabling you to participate more fully in daily activities, work, and leisure pursuits.

By engaging in these adaptive strategies, you can better navigate your daily life, maintain your independence, and improve your overall quality of life.

Developing Your Own Adaptive Strategies

Now that you see the power of adaptation, it's time to better personalize this technique. Identify a specific daily task or activity that presents a challenge due to your disability. Research and implement an adaptive strategy, tool, or modification that can assist you in overcoming this challenge. Practice using the adaptive strategy and track your progress.

Reflections:

Describe how the adaptive strategy or tool you want to implement can improve your ability to perform the task or activity.

_____

_____.

Reflect on any changes you anticipate—or actually gain—with regard to your independence, confidence, or overall well-being as a result of utilizing adaptive strategies.

_____

_____

_____.

Additional Reflections on Adaptive Strategies

How can assistive technology enhance your independence and quality of life?

_____

_____

_____.

What modifications can be made to your living space to improve accessibility and convenience?

_____

_____

_____.

In what ways can adaptive clothing support your comfort and personal
style while accommodating your disability?

_____

_____

_____.

Are there any adaptive sports or recreational activities that interest you?
How can you get involved in these activities within your community?

_____

_____

_____.

Living with a disability requires a holistic approach that addresses physical,
emotional, and financial aspects. By acknowledging the emotional journey,
seeking support, and exploring adaptive strategies, you can empower yourself to overcome challenges and thrive. Remember Christopher Powell's
advice in *Bounce Back*: set goals, maintain your resilience, and don't let
yourself get too emotionally high or too low.

Recall too that Christopher, who was wheelchair-bound as a quadriple-
gic, learned to walk and even run races. How would you feel about trying
such a feat—or doing anything sports-related outside of your normal physical comfort zone?

Reflections on Adaptive Sports

How do you feel about the idea of participating in adaptive sports or recreational activities in a public setting? Are there any specific emotions
that arise?

_____

_____

_____.

What would excite you, if anything, about engaging in adaptive sports or recreational activities?

_____

_____

_____.

What fears or concerns, if any, would make you hesitant about participating in adaptive sports or recreational activities?

_____

_____

_____.

Are there any support systems or strategies you can put in place to address any concerns, including any anticipated or potential emotional or physical discomfort?

_____

_____

_____.

Hopefully, this chapter has shown you numerous ways that your disability can be managed emotionally, physically, and financially. Keep pressing forward, knowing that like all Dreaded Ds, having a disability is a challenge—but one that doesn't have to diminish your life or happiness.

As we conclude this sixth chapter of *The Bounce Back Workbook*, which focused on disability, take time to think about what you have just done, felt, and discovered. What emotions surfaced for you during the exercises? What lessons have you learned so far, and what growth have you experienced? Write a recap below.

_____

_____

_____

_____

Chapter 7

Disease

Chronic diseases, such as heart disease, cancer, and diabetes, affect millions of individuals and their families, posing significant challenges to both health and finances. Even if you don't have a chronic condition, even facing a one-time battle with a disease can be sobering. So in this chapter, we'll address the various aspects of coping with a disease, guide you through practical steps to manage your health, communicate effectively with health care providers, and navigate the financial implications that often accompany disease. As always, the goal is to empower you to overcome challenges, prioritize self-care, and find financial stability amid the specific Dreaded D.

Managing Emotional Well-being

To keep yourself healthy and whole, explore different self-care practices that promote emotional well-being, such as mindfulness exercises, journaling, or engaging in hobbies or activities that bring you joy. Try to incorporate at least one self-care practice into your daily routine for a week and track the impact on your emotional well-being.

Reflection questions:

What self-care practices have you found helpful in managing stress and promoting emotional well-being?

_____

_____.

How can you prioritize self-care while balancing the financial challenges of your disease?

_____

_____.

How can you create a supportive environment for your emotional well-being while navigating the financial implications of the disease?

_____

_____.

Building a Support System

When you have an illness or disease, you need to identify the people in your life that you can turn to for support during challenging times. You should also have a clear understanding of how they can—and in some cases cannot—assist you emotionally, physically, or even financially.

Reflection questions:

Have you sought emotional support or counseling to help you navigate the emotional toll of your disease? If not, what are the barriers that prevent you from seeking professional help?

_____

_____.

Are you connected with support groups or online communities where you can share experiences and find understanding from others facing similar health challenges? If not, what steps can you take to find and join these communities?

_____

_____.

Strengthening Your Support System

At every phase of your disease or illness, it helps to have cheerleaders in your corner. So even if you're doing well one day with the physical aspects of your disease, or with the financial and emotional side, it pays to have a select number of go-to individuals just to talk to when needed.

Reach out to a support group or online community specific to your disease or health condition. Introduce yourself and share your experiences, challenges, and triumphs.

Engage in conversations with others who can provide support, advice, and encouragement.

Reflection questions:

Who are the trusted people in your life who have been supportive throughout your disease journey? How have they made a positive impact?

_____

_____.

In what ways can you actively seek out and connect with others who have gone through similar experiences?

_____

_____.

How can you build and nurture a strong support system that will help you in good and challenging times?

_____

_____.

What kind of support do you need from your loved ones, friends, or community to navigate the financial challenges of your disease?

_____

_____.

Schedule time to have any necessary conversations to let family or friends know your needs.

Navigating the Financial and Emotional Challenges

As mentioned, dealing with disease and chronic health conditions can be overwhelming, both emotionally and financially. When you or a loved one is diagnosed with a disease, it often brings a flood of medical bills that can feel never-ending. Even if you physically recover, the financial burden can persist long after your treatments end. However, it's important to remember that you can regain both your physical and fiscal health. Here are some questions to help you navigate the challenges that come with disease.

Activity: Facing the Financial Impact

How has the diagnosis of a disease affected your financial situation? What are the specific economic challenges you're facing?

_____

_____.

What steps have you taken so far to address the financial burden of your medical bills? Are there any strategies or resources you've found helpful?

_____

_____.

How does the financial aspect of your disease impact your overall well-being? What emotions or concerns does it bring up for you?

_____

_____.

Handling Lost Income and Employment Challenges

Having a disease can impact your ability to work or create the need for limitations and accommodations in order to preserve your well-being. Naturally, you may be concerned about sharing certain medical information with an employer if you feel your job could be on the line. But it's important to get the right support, resources, and necessary accommodations you need. Otherwise, you're potentially setting yourself up for a physically and emotionally taxing scenario that is simply unsustainable.

Reflection questions:

Have you explored workplace accommodations or flexibility options? If not, what steps can you take to initiate that conversation with your employer?

_____

_____.

What alternative work arrangements, such as freelancing or part-time work, could be suitable for you considering your health needs? How might these options impact your financial situation?

_____

_____.

In assessing your work abilities and limitations, create a list of your routine job tasks and responsibilities and evaluate how your illness may impact your ability to perform each task effectively. Consider consulting with a vocational rehabilitation specialist or career counselor to assess your work abilities and limitations.

Reflection questions:

How does your illness affect your physical, cognitive, or emotional capabilities in a work environment?

_____

_____.

What adjustments or accommodations do you believe would be most beneficial for you in the workplace?

_____

_____.

How comfortable do you feel discussing your illness and accommodation needs with your employer or human resources department?

_____

_____.

How can you effectively communicate your accommodation requests to ensure a supportive work environment?

_____

_____.

How comfortable and prepared would you be to explore alternative employment options?

_____

_____.

Research the Americans with Disabilities Act (ADA) guidelines to understand your rights regarding workplace accommodations. Identifying specific accommodations that could enhance your productivity and well-being in the workplace will help you on a current or future job.

Assessing Your Financial Situation

When you're facing a pile of health-related expenses, it can seem like the only thing that comes in the mail are bills, bills, and more bills! Take a breather and resolve to sort out all the financial paperwork. You can do this. Here are some pointers to help.

Create a comprehensive list of all your medical expenses, including bills, insurance statements, and out-of-pocket costs. Organize them by category (e.g. hospital bills, medication costs). Then calculate the total amount spent on health care and compare it to your income or financial resources.

Look at ways to cut costs or negotiate with health care providers to lower your health care expenses. For example, can you switch that brand name medication or prescription drug to a generic? Can you contact the office manager or doctor at the clinic you visited and see if they'll accept a lower amount than what's on the bill? It never hurts to ask for a reduced fee when it comes to health care costs. And many physicians and health care providers will cut you a deal when you pay for services in cash.

Reflection questions:

Reflect on the financial impact of the disease on your life. How has illness or disease affected your income, expenses, and overall financial
stability?

_____

_____.

What are the specific challenges you have faced, and how have they influenced your financial well-being?

_____

_____.

What adjustments have you made to accommodate the financial strain of
the disease?

_____

_____.

How does the financial burden of the disease impact your daily life and
long-term goals?

_____

_____.

What emotions arise when you think about the financial implications of
your disease? How do these emotions influence your decision-making
process?

_____

_____.

Setting Realistic Financial Goals

We all want to live a life unburdened by debt, and that includes medical
debt. If you have past-due medical bills, you may be longing for a fresh
start and a way from underneath all those hefty health care expenses. And

I don't blame you. The stress of medical bills is enough to make you have to see the doctor—causing *more* bills!

So let's start to envision a future without health care bills hanging over your head.

Identify three short-term financial goals related to your disease recovery. Write down specific actions you will take to achieve these goals, such as creating a budget, exploring financial assistance programs, or negotiating medical bills.

Goal #1: _____

Goal #2: _____

Goal #3: _____

Action step #1: _____

Action step #2: _____

Action step #3: _____

How can setting financial goals help you regain a sense of control and stability in your life?

_____

_____.

What resources or support do you need to achieve these goals?

_____

_____.

Communication with Health Care Providers

It may seem daunting to have to deal with doctors, health care companies, insurance firms, and more—all while you're trying to look after your own health. But there's no getting around it: communication with all of these individuals and entities is a necessary part of navigating your illness and getting what you need.

So prepare a list of questions or concerns you have about your disease, treatment options, or financial aspects of your health care. Practice role-playing scenarios with a trusted friend or family member, where they play the role of a health care provider, and you practice communicating your questions or concerns effectively. Do what it takes to get confident advocating for yourself.

Reflections on Your Communication and Advocacy

How comfortable do you feel advocating for yourself and communicating your needs to health care providers? Is speaking up easy or hard for you? Why?

_____

_____.

What strategies can you implement to improve your communication skills and ensure that your concerns are addressed?

_____

_____.

What barriers or challenges have you encountered when trying to communicate your financial concerns to health care professionals? How can you overcome these obstacles?

_____

_____.

Effective Communication and Advocacy

Only you know how comfortable you are with communicating your needs and concerns to health care providers. If there any specific challenges you face in advocating for yourself, now is the time to address those challenges—or work out other solutions where others can advocate on your behalf.

Reflection questions:

How familiar are you with billing and insurance terminology? What areas do you feel uncertain about, and how can you educate yourself to better understand your financial responsibilities?

_____

_____.

Have you explored the possibility of payment plans or negotiating with health care providers to manage your medical bills? If not, what are the reasons holding you back, and how can you overcome them?

_____

_____.

Write down the names of three relatives or friends you can enlist to help you deal with medical bills.

Family member/friend #1: _____

Family member/friend #2: _____

Family member/friend #3: _____

   Remember, these activities are meant to help you reflect on your personal situation and take proactive steps toward managing the financial and emotional challenges of your disease. Use them as a starting point to develop strategies and seek support that can assist you in regaining both your physical and fiscal well-being.

Navigating Medical Billing and Insurance

Tackling your insurance concerns is another top financial matter when you have a disease or illness. To better deal with this scenario, get into the habit of reviewing your medical bills or insurance statements and identifying any errors, discrepancies, or unclear charges. If you feel more comfortable taking a test run, practice writing a letter or email to the billing department or insurance company, addressing your concerns and seeking clarification.

Then, when you're confident you've expressed everything that needs to be said—from your treatment to your costs—fire away and send the real email or letter. Don't worry about hurting anyone's feelings. Keep your tone and requests polite but firm. Part of advocating for yourself is letting people know when things go wrong and insisting that they be corrected. Also review my advice in the chapter on disaster recovery in *Bounce Back*. Even though that's a completely different topic, I offer tips that are relevant here for how to handle the two most common insurance problems: having inadequate documentation and needing an advocate on your side. You can pick up some insurance-related nuggets of wisdom that can be applied in this scenario.

Reflection questions:

How confident do you feel when reviewing medical bills and insurance statements?

_____

_____.

What steps can you take to ensure that you understand your medical billing and insurance coverage?

_____

_____.

How can you advocate for yourself when faced with billing errors or challenges?

_____

_____.

How does the complexity of medical billing and insurance impact your overall financial well-being and stress levels?

_____

_____.

How can you develop a proactive approach to managing your medical bills and understanding your insurance coverage?

_____

_____.

Have you ever faced a denial from your health insurer? If so, how did you navigate the appeals process?

_____

_____.

What resources or support can you tap into for guidance and assistance in appealing a denial?

_____

_____.

How can persistence, organization, and advocacy contribute to a successful outcome when appealing a denial from your health insurer?

_____

_____.

Addressing Billing Issues and Disputing Medical Bills

It may be helpful to create a template or a rough sample letter to dispute a medical bill and request adjustments or corrections. Then you can use the template as an outline for future disputes. Research your local consumer protection laws and regulations regarding medical billing and debt too. There are both federal and state guidelines covering the activities and billing practices for health care companies, insurers, and other institutions that deal with consumers.

Reflection questions:

Have you ever disputed a medical bill? If so, what was your experience like?

_____

_____.

How comfortable do you feel with asserting your rights and disputing medical bills with health care providers?

_____

_____.

What concerns or fears do you have about the potential consequences of disputing medical bills?

_____

_____.

How comfortable do you feel sharing your own experiences or stories about medical debt?

_____

_____.

What benefits or impact can sharing personal stories have on individuals facing medical debt?

_____

_____.

How can sharing personal stories contribute to raising awareness, reducing stigma, and advocating for change?

_____

_____.

Remember to approach these activities, exercises, and reflections at your own pace and adapt them to your unique circumstances. Seek assistance from patient advocates, health care lawyers, or support groups if needed. By building your knowledge, advocating for yourself, and effectively communicating with health care providers and insurance companies, you can navigate the health care system with confidence and ensure you receive the care and coverage you deserve.

Understanding Charity Care Programs

Recall that in *Bounce Back*, I explained that charity care programs at hospitals and health care systems are supposed to offer free or steeply discounted services to eligible patients. Unfortunately, far too many qualified patients still get billed for services that rightfully ought to have been free, based on the individual's income or asset level. Don't let this happen to you. Do some basic research and gather information on charity care programs offered by hospitals and health care systems in your area. Then create a list of eligibility criteria and application processes for charity care programs.

Reflection questions:

Have you ever explored or utilized charity care programs? If not, what barriers or hesitations have prevented you from doing so?

_____

_____.

How confident are you in navigating the application process for charity care programs?

_____

_____.

What questions or concerns do you have about the limitations or potential drawbacks of charity care programs?

_____

_____.

How can charity care programs provide relief and support for individuals facing medical debt?

_____

_____.

What steps can you take to ensure that you meet the eligibility criteria and successfully apply for charity care programs?

_____

_____.

How can you advocate for improvements or changes to charity care programs to ensure equitable access to health care services?

_____

_____.

The Movement to Abolish Medical Debt

Finally, if you are struggling with medical debt due to illness or disease, you should know about a growing movement in America to abolish medical debt outright. At the forefront of the movement is a nonprofit organization called RIP Medical Debt, which buys medical debt in bulk for pennies on the dollar and then forgives it. The organization uses donations to buy up debt and then abolish it, effectively removing the burden on those in need. Since its founding, RIP Medical Debt has abolished more than $10 billion in medical debt.

RIP Medical Debt, founded in 2014 by former debt collection agents, has been uniquely successful in its approach to medical debt relief. They negotiate directly with hospitals or hospital systems to buy large portfolios of medical debt for pennies on the dollar and then cancel the debt en masse. This model has been increasingly adopted by local governments as a way to provide economic relief to their constituents, with cities such as Cleveland and Toledo, Ohio, as well as Cook County, Illinois, using funds from the American Rescue Plan Act (COVID funds) to contract with RIP Medical Debt and clear hundreds of millions in medical debt for their residents.

RIP Medical Debt has also benefited from substantial donations, including $80 million from philanthropist MacKenzie Scott, which they have used to create an internal revolving line of credit. This allows the organization to buy debt portfolios from hospitals before securing specific funding to cover the cost, providing flexibility and enabling expansion.

Churches and Faith-based Organizations
Abolish Debt Too

There have been several instances where churches or faith-based organizations have also raised funds to buy and forgive medical debt. For example, in 2019, a church in Texas wiped out over $10 million in medical debt for local residents. The church partnered with RIP Medical Debt to buy up the debt for pennies on the dollar and then forgave it. In 2020, Crossroads Church, which is based in Cincinnati, Ohio, bought up and then forgave $46 million in medical debt, helping 45,000 people in the area. More recently, in March 2023, the congregation of Trinity Moravian Church in Winston-Salem, North Carolina, announced that it had purchased $3.3 million worth of medical debt that belonged to 3,355 local families, all at a fraction of its original cost. The church's celebration was filled with joyous bells ringing and confetti flying as they hosted a "debt burning" ceremony, symbolizing the complete forgiveness of these burdensome debts.

In the latter case, this transformative achievement was made possible through the coordination of donations totaling just over $15,000, facilitated by the church's Debt Jubilee Project in collaboration with RIP Medical Debt. With initiatives such as the Debt Jubilee Project gaining momentum, more churches across the United States are uniting to provide substantial relief to community members burdened by debt. Church leaders emphasize that debt forgiveness, a modern yet highly effective approach, aligns firmly with the teachings of scripture and the pursuit of doing good for others.

Additionally, sites such as GoFundMe have become a popular way for individuals to raise money to pay off their medical debts. While this doesn't necessarily involve buying debt in bulk, it is a way that communities can come together using crowdfunding to help individuals in need.

Be aware, too, that some hospitals and health care providers offer medical debt resolution programs, which can involve negotiating down the debt or setting up payment plans that are more manageable for patients. These programs are often income-based and may be available to those who are uninsured or underinsured.

As mentioned earlier, some nonprofit hospitals and health care providers also offer charity care programs, which provide free or reduced-cost care to eligible individuals. These programs can help prevent medical debt from accruing in the first place.

Collectively, these are just a few examples of the ways that organizations and communities are working to tackle the problem of medical debt. It's a complex issue that requires innovative solutions, and these programs represent some of the ways that people are trying to help. However, it's also important to note that these programs can't completely solve the issue on their own, and broader systemic changes are likely needed to fully address the problem of medical debt in America.

As we conclude this seventh chapter of *The Bounce Back Workbook*, which focused on disease, take time to think about what you have just done, felt, and discovered. What emotions surfaced for you during the exercises? What lessons have you learned so far, and what growth have you experienced? Write a recap below.

_____

_____

_____

_____

_____

Chapter 8

Disasters

Wildfires. Tornadoes. Earthquakes. Hurricanes. Floods. All these natural disasters can threaten your physical and financial well-being. When a powerful natural disaster strikes, you may be happy simply to have escaped with your life. But the shock, emotional blow, and financial ramifications of potentially losing life or property can often make it hard to know what to do first. Fortunately, experts and those who have survived Mother Nature's wrath offer great insights into how you can prepare for and deal with the aftermath of catastrophic climate events.

Whether you have experienced a disaster firsthand or want to be prepared for potential future events, this chapter is designed to empower you to overcome nature's fury, bounce back, and create a more resilient future. Use this *Workbook* as your guide, offering you the tools, information, resources, and support you need to navigate the challenges of devastating disasters, rebuild your life, and create a stable path forward.

Your Experience with Disaster

Reflect on the most significant natural disaster or extreme weather event that has affected your life or the lives of people you know. Write a journal entry or create a visual representation depicting the emotional and financial impact of the disaster.

How did the natural disaster or extreme weather event impact you or your community?

_____

_____.

What were the immediate challenges and long-term consequences you faced as a result?

_____

_____.

How did going through this disaster shape your perspective on preparedness and resilience?

_____

_____.

Reflections on Preparedness

How did the natural disaster or extreme weather event affect your sense of safety and security?

_____

_____.

Based on your experience, what would you do differently (or the same) if a similar disaster hit?

_____

_____.

Preparing for and Coping with Natural Disasters

Developing a personal emergency plan for yourself and your family, including steps to take before, during, and after a natural disaster is vital for your safety and well-being. You should also create an emergency kit with essential supplies and keep it readily accessible in case of a disaster. Your safety plans should account for the threats that are most common or typical in your region. For instance, if you live in a flood-prone area, you should know the best evacuation route to avoid (to the best extent possible) major flood zones. Additionally, your emergency kit should contain items that serve the specific needs of you and your family. For example, if you have pets, you might have a separate emergency kit just for them. Here's a checklist of 20 essential items to consider including in an emergency preparedness kit, followed by some planning tips and a checklist of what to include in an emergency kit for pets.

Checklist of 20 Essential Items in an Emergency Kit

Water: Have at least one gallon of water per person per day for a minimum of three days.

Non-perishable food: Stock up on canned or dry foods that don't require refrigeration or cooking, and consider dietary needs.

Manual can opener: To open canned food items.

Flashlights: Include extra batteries or opt for hand-cranked flashlights.

First-aid kit: Include bandages, antiseptic ointment, pain relievers, and any necessary prescription medications.

Battery-powered or hand-cranked radio: To stay informed about emergency updates.

Whistle: Use for signaling for help.

Multi-purpose tool: A Swiss Army knife or a multi-tool can be useful in various situations.

Personal hygiene items: Include items such as soap, toothpaste, toothbrushes, and toilet paper.

Cell phone charger: Have a portable charger or a solar-powered charger.

Extra clothing and blankets: Pack extra clothes, sturdy shoes, and blankets for warmth.

Cash: Keep a decent amount of cash ($200 to $500) in case of power outages or if electronic transactions are unavailable.

Important documents: Have copies of identification, insurance policies, medical records, and contact information in a waterproof container or a secure digital format.

Emergency contact list: Write down important phone numbers and addresses of family members, friends, and local emergency services.

Maps: Include a local map and a map of your area or region.

Emergency shelter: Consider a tent or a tarp for temporary shelter if needed.

Duct tape and plastic sheeting: Can be used for emergency repairs and sealing windows.

Extra batteries: Include spare batteries for your flashlight and other battery-powered devices.

Sanitation supplies: Include items such as moist towelettes, garbage bags, and plastic ties for personal sanitation.

Entertainment items: Include books, puzzles, cards, or other activities to help pass the time and reduce stress.

Remember to periodically check and update your emergency kit, especially food, water, and medications, to ensure they are not expired. Customize the kit based on your specific needs and location.

Planning for Your Pets Before Disaster Strikes

Just as it is essential for us humans to prepare for and respond to disasters, it is equally crucial to plan for and tend to the needs of our animal companions and pets before weather events or emergencies strike. Our pets rely on us for their well-being and safety, and incorporating them into our emergency preparedness plans ensures their welfare. This involves identifying pet-friendly shelters or alternative accommodations, assembling a dedicated emergency kit for our pets, and keeping their identification and medical records up to date.

By acknowledging the responsibility we have toward our furry friends and taking proactive measures to address their needs, we can help ensure their safety and comfort during challenging times, and give ourselves peace of mind knowing that we are fully prepared to care for them during emergencies. Here's a checklist of things to do and items to have for pets as part of your emergency preparedness plan.

Pet Planning and Preparedness Checklist

Identification: Ensure your pets have identification tags with up-to-date contact information.

Microchip: Consider microchipping your pets and registering their information in a national database.

Emergency contacts: Keep a list of emergency contacts, including your veterinarian's contact information and nearby animal shelters or pet-friendly hotels.

Pet-friendly shelters: Research pet-friendly shelters in your area or have a plan in place with friends or family who can accommodate your pets if evacuation is necessary.

Evacuation routes: Familiarize yourself with evacuation routes and destinations that allow pets.

Emergency kit: Prepare a separate emergency kit specifically for your pets, including the items in the following list.

Checklist of Essential Supplies for Your Pet's Emergency Kit

Food and water: Pack at least a three-day supply of pet food in an airtight, waterproof container. Also, include bottled water and bowls for drinking.

Medications and medical records: Keep a supply of any necessary medications your pet requires and have a copy of their medical records in a waterproof bag.

Pet first-aid kit: Include basic first-aid supplies, such as bandages, antiseptic solution, and any specific items recommended by your veterinarian.

Leashes, collars, and harnesses: Have sturdy leashes, collars, and harnesses for each pet.

Carriers and/or crates: Provide secure and comfortable carriers or crates for each pet, large enough for them to stand, turn around, and lie down.

Comfort items: Pack familiar bedding, toys, and comfort items to help reduce stress for your pets during an emergency.

Sanitation supplies: Include poop bags, litter, a litter box, and cleaning supplies for proper pet waste disposal.

Recent photo: Keep a recent photo of each pet in case they become lost.

Calming aids: If your pet is prone to anxiety, include items such as calming treats, anxiety wraps, or pheromone sprays.

Pet care instructions: Prepare written instructions outlining your pet's feeding schedule, medication regimen, behavior quirks, and any other essential information for anyone caring for your pet during an emergency.

Pet carrier stickers: Attach stickers or decals to your home's windows or doors indicating the number and type of pets inside to alert emergency responders.

Familiar smells: Place an item with your scent or the scent of home in the pet carrier to provide comfort.

Familiar environment: If possible, bring a small piece of your pet's familiar bedding or a favorite toy to help them feel more secure.

Practice and familiarize: Train and familiarize your pets with their carriers and emergency procedures to minimize stress during an actual emergency.

Remember to review and update your pet's emergency kit regularly, including food, medications, and any necessary documents. Make sure to consider the specific needs of your pets and adjust the checklist accordingly. For example, my family has two beagles—Astro and Comet. We know that Astro hates loud noises, and he gets scared by things such as thunder. So he prefers to go inside his crate when major storms occur in our area.

Reflection questions

What are the specific natural disasters or extreme weather events that pose a threat in your area?

_____

_____.

How can you ensure the safety and well-being of your loved ones/pets during a natural disaster?

_____

_____

_____

_____.

Have you identified safe locations or evacuation routes in your community in case of an emergency? If so, write a quick summary of those locations and routes.

_____

_____.

If you have a business, what steps have you taken to protect your infrastructure or operations?

_____

_____.

What more can you do to ensure you have an optimal level of disaster preparedness?

_____

_____.

Partnerships and Local-led Efforts in Disaster Recovery

As mentioned, it takes all of us to help achieve effective disaster recovery in the wake of a powerful disaster. You can play a role in ensuring your and your neighbors' safety by identifying and researching local organizations or initiatives involved in disaster recovery efforts in your community. You can also volunteer or participate in local disaster preparedness or recovery programs.

Reflection questions:

What gifts or talents do you have that might support disaster recovery efforts at the local level?

_____

_____.

In your area, are there any specific challenges or gaps in current disaster recovery programs that need to be addressed?

_____

_____.

How can you contribute to or advocate for building a resilient and inclusive community that is prepared to respond to and recover from disasters?

_____

_____.

In what ways can you get involved in volunteering or supporting your community during and after a disaster?

_____

_____.

Developing Your Emergency Contact List

A final essential part of emergency planning is knowing where to turn—quickly—for needed help and support. So it's important to create an emergency contact list that includes important numbers for emergency services, insurance companies, local authorities, and family members.

The following is a checklist to help you get started. Write down the phone numbers for each contact in this *Workbook*, but also transfer the contact information to your cell phone, emergency kit, and the cloud to have this info handy if disaster strikes. (Alternatively, once you're done reading it, you could also keep this copy of *The Bounce Back Workbook* in your emergency kit too!)

Checklist of Emergency Services, Organizations, and People for Disaster Planning

Local emergency services: Research and note down the phone numbers for your local police, fire department, and ambulance service. These numbers are typically available through local directories or online resources.

Police: _____

Fire Department: _____

Ambulance: _____

Other: _____

National emergency services: Familiarize yourself with the emergency hotline number in your country. For example, in the United States, Canada, and Mexico, the emergency hotline is 911. In other countries, it varies: India uses 112, Brazil 190, and South Africa 10111. Meanwhile, the United Kingdom uses 999, and the European Union uses 112. So be sure to know the appropriate number for your location.

Local government agencies: Identify the phone numbers for your local government offices responsible for disaster response and emergency management. This may include agencies such as emergency management departments, public safety departments, or civil defense offices.

_____

_____

_____

_____

Animal control services: Keep contact information for local animal control services or animal welfare organizations that can assist with the evacuation or care of animals during emergencies.

_____

_____

Nonemergency police line: In situations where immediate response may not be required, having the nonemergency police line number can be helpful to report nonurgent incidents or seek guidance.

_____

Poison control center: Save the number for your regional poison control center, which can provide guidance on potential poisoning emergencies involving humans or pets.

_____

Local health services: Note down the contact information for local health services, such as hospitals, clinics, or health departments, for medical emergencies or health-related concerns during disasters.

_____

_____

_____

_____

Electric and gas companies: Have the phone numbers for your electricity and gas providers readily available to report utility outages, gas leaks, or other related emergencies.

Electric company: _____

Gas company: _____

Water and sewage services: Keep the contact information for your local water and sewage utilities to report water supply issues or sewage problems.

Water Company: _____

Sewage Service: _____

Local Red Cross chapter: Find the phone number for your local Red Cross chapter(s), as they often provide emergency assistance, shelter, and support during disasters.

_____

_____

Road and highway assistance: Note the number of roadside assistance or highway patrol agencies that can offer help in case of road closures, accidents, or other transportation-related emergencies.

_____

_____

National Weather Service: Stay informed about weather conditions and warnings by having the phone number of your local National Weather Service office or the designated meteorological authority in your country.

_____

_____

Insurance providers: Keep the contact information for your insurance companies readily available to report any damages or initiate insurance claims in the aftermath of a natural disaster.

_____

_____

Local community organizations: Identify local community organizations or volunteer groups involved in disaster response or relief efforts, as they may offer support or resources during emergencies.

_____

_____

Nearby neighbors and family: Have the contact information for nearby neighbors, family members, or friends who can provide assistance or support during emergencies.

_____

_____

_____

_____

Again, remember to program these numbers into your mobile phone and keep a hard copy of the list in your emergency kit. You can also keep a copy posted in a visible location at home. Additionally, check with your local emergency management agency for any region-specific contacts or resources that may be relevant to your area.

Securing Federal Disaster Recovery Assistance

Getting the help you need after a disaster can sometimes feel like an impossible task when paperwork, slow systems, or bureaucratic processes bring everything to a grind. However, it's important to remember that there are resources available to help. Also, everyone has a role to play in the recovery process following a natural disaster, including you, other community members, government, public and private agencies, nonprofits, and more.

Getting assistance from the Federal Emergency Management Agency (FEMA) can be crucial when you've been affected by disasters. To begin the process, you should register with FEMA by either calling their toll-free number (800-621-3362) or applying online through the FEMA website at FEMA.gov. (The FEMA contact info is TTY 1-800-462-7585 for the speech- or hearing-impaired.) Once registered, FEMA may provide you with financial assistance for various disaster-related needs, such as temporary housing, home repairs, and other disaster-related expenses not covered by insurance. To ensure a smooth application process, it's important to have the following checklist of documents and information readily available when applying for FEMA aid:

FEMA Application Checklist

Social Security number: You will need to provide your Social Security number or that of a household member.

Address and insurance information: Have your current address and details of your insurance coverage on hand.

Description of damage and losses: Be prepared to provide a detailed description of the damages and losses you have incurred due to the disaster.

Contact information: Provide accurate contact details, including your current phone number and mailing address.

Proof of ownership and residency: Prepare to present documents such as property titles, lease agreements, or utility bills that establish your ownership or residency.

Financial information: Gather income details for all household members, including pay stubs, bank statements, or tax records.

Bank account information: Have your bank account details available for direct deposit of FEMA assistance funds, if eligible.

Temporary residence information: If you are temporarily staying in a different location, provide the address and contact information for your temporary residence.

Documentation of disaster assistance from other sources: If you have received assistance from other sources, such as insurance or charitable organizations, provide any relevant documentation.

Medical and funeral expenses: If you have incurred medical or funeral expenses due to the disaster, gather related documents and receipts.

Other documentation: Include any additional documentation related to your specific circumstances, such as photographs of damages or written estimates for repairs.

By having this checklist of necessary documents and information readily available, you can streamline the FEMA application process and increase your chances of receiving timely and appropriate assistance to aid in your disaster recovery efforts.

Reflection questions:

Have you or anyone you know ever received federal or government disaster recovery assistance? What was the experience like?

_____

_____

What challenges or barriers did you encounter when seeking disaster
recovery assistance?

_____

_____.

Are you aware of any local or community-based organizations that provide support to individuals affected by natural disasters? If so, list
them below.

_____

_____

_____

_____.

Don't Forget Self-care and Connection

During times of disaster, it's crucial to prioritize your emotional well-being
and practice self-care to navigate through the challenges with resilience and
compassion for yourself. It's normal to feel overwhelmed, anxious, or scared
during such difficult times. Be gentle with yourself and allow yourself to
experience and process your emotions. Take breaks when needed, finding
moments of calm and grounding amid the chaos. Engage in activities that
bring you comfort and relaxation, whether it's listening to soothing music,
practicing deep breathing exercises, taking walks, or indulging in a favorite
hobby. Connect with loved ones, sharing your thoughts and feelings with
those who provide support and understanding. Seek solace in moments
of self-reflection and introspection, allowing yourself to acknowledge your
strength and resilience. Remember, self-care is not selfish; it's essential for
your well-being and to help you manage stress as you navigate the aftermath of a disaster.

It can also help to band together with others who have gone through the
same thing that you're experiencing. So engage with your neighbors, attend
community meetings, participate in local support groups, and consider volunteering for recovery efforts too. Seeing others in the same plight—and
perhaps worse—may give you a greater sense of gratitude and renewed
faith that, together, you can all overcome this challenge.

Reflection questions:

How has the emotional impact of the disaster impacted you? Reflect on any changes you've noticed in your mental well-being and coping strategies.

_____

_____.

What resources or support networks can you tap into to address ongoing mental health concerns?

_____

_____.

How can you incorporate self-care practices into your daily routine to support your emotional well-being?

_____

_____.

What creative solutions or alternatives can you explore to improve your living situation if your housing has been disrupted?

_____

_____.

Addressing Financial and Insurance Concerns

If you've suffered property damage as a result of an Act of God—as insurance companies call natural disasters—you'll have to contact your insurers to file a claim. Approach the process with a clear and organized mindset. Start by reviewing your insurance policy thoroughly to understand the coverage and claim procedures. Document all damages extensively, taking photos and keeping a detailed inventory of affected items. Contact your insurance company promptly to report the claim and provide accurate and comprehensive information. Keep records of all communication, including dates, names, and details discussed. Be proactive and follow up regularly to ensure progress is being made. Familiarize yourself with your rights as a policyholder, and seek guidance from a public adjuster or insurance claims attorney in your area if needed. Patience and persistence are key, as the process may take time. Remember to remain calm, assertive, and professional during all interactions.

Disaster recovery and emergency management expert Chris Burt, who has worked at FEMA and is now a Disaster Program Manager with the Red Cross, says the two most important things to do financially are to have sufficient savings to be able to pay any required money toward your insurance deductibles and have good documentation of your losses.

"Take pictures: that's always helpful because they tell the story," Burt says. "Keep receipts. Take videos. Have as much information as possible. The insurance company may or may not ask you for it. But if you ever have to contest a decision, depending on what your policy says, the burden of proof is always on you."

Indeed, some insurance carriers are increasingly staying away from disaster-prone areas. For instance, State Farm and Allstate both announced in 2023 that they stopped selling homeowners insurance in California because of the rise in construction costs and increased disasters, such as wildfires, in the Golden State.

Special Considerations for Immigrants and Undocumented Individuals

Burt also notes that disasters hit communities of color and immigrants disproportionately. The latter face very specific concerns when it comes to insurance and disaster recovery. Undocumented individuals or immigrants without legal status in the US may find difficulty in obtaining property insurance, as many insurance companies require applicants to provide a valid Social Security number or taxpayer identification number. However, some insurance companies may offer alternatives or options for individuals without legal status. It's advisable for undocumented individuals to consult with local insurance agents or brokers who can provide specific information about available options. In some cases, there may be insurance programs or policies specifically designed for underserved populations that could be accessible.

Additionally, exploring community organizations or immigrant advocacy groups may offer guidance and resources for finding suitable insurance options or connecting with relevant agencies that can provide aid. Burt says groups such as Catholic Charities, the Red Cross, and the Salvation Army all help individuals regardless of their residency or legal status.

Reflection questions:

Imagine your insurance claim is denied or the payout offered is insufficient. How would you advocate for yourself in such a situation?

_____

_____.

What steps would you take to seek professional help and navigate the legal aspects of the claims process?

_____

_____.

Natural disasters can have devastating effects on you, your family, and your community. They disrupt lives, damage property, and challenge our sense of security. Even though natural disasters are undeniably incredibly challenging, they also provide an opportunity for growth, community support, and the chance to create a better future. By embracing the lessons contained in this chapter, taking proactive steps, and working together for the collective good, you can build your resilience and create a safer and more secure environment for yourself and those around you.

As we conclude this eighth chapter of _The Bounce Back Workbook_, which focused on disasters, take time to think about what you have just done, felt, and discovered. What emotions surfaced for you during the exercises? What lessons have you learned so far, and what growth have you experienced? Write a recap below.

_____

_____

_____

_____

Chapter 9

Debt

D ebt can feel overwhelming and suffocating, affecting not only your financial health but also your emotional and mental well-being. Whether you are burdened by credit card debt, student loans, or other forms of debt, this chapter of *The Bounce Back Workbook* is designed to empower you to break free from the cycle of debt and create a solid foundation for financial well-being. Developing repayment plans and committing to regular payments not only reduces your overall debt burden but also boosts your confidence and sense of accomplishment.

Recognizing Emotional Spending

In our everyday lives, each of us tends to engage in emotional spending, often without even realizing it. This phenomenon occurs when our emotions influence our purchasing decisions, leading us down a path that can ultimately result in credit card debt. Emotions such as stress, happiness, sadness, or even boredom can trigger impulsive buying behaviors. When you feel stressed or overwhelmed, you may seek comfort in "retail therapy," purchasing items to momentarily lift your spirits. Similarly, when you're happy or celebrating an accomplishment, you may be more inclined to splurge on extravagant purchases as a way to reward yourself. On the other hand, during times of sadness or loneliness, you might turn to shopping as a temporary escape from negative feelings. Additionally, sheer boredom can lead you to engage in retail therapy, as shopping can provide a sense of excitement or novelty.

Unfortunately, these emotional spending sprees can have detrimental consequences, particularly when you rely on credit cards to finance your purchases. The instant gratification provided by emotional spending can quickly fade, leaving you with mounting credit card bills and a burden that can take time to overcome. It is crucial to be mindful of your emotional state when making purchasing decisions and develop healthier coping mechanisms to avoid falling into the trap of emotional spending and the resulting credit card debt.

Activity: Identifying Your Emotional Spending Triggers

Take a moment to reflect on your spending habits and consider the emotions that drive your purchases. Write below about the ways in which your emotions may drive your spending.

Think about the last few times you made impulsive purchases or spent money to cope with emotions. What were the circumstances surrounding those instances? Were you feeling stressed, anxious, sad, bored, or something else? What did you buy?

_____

_____.

Write down the emotions that commonly trigger your impulsive spending. Be honest with yourself and try to identify recurring patterns.

_____

_____.

Consider any specific situations, environments, or triggers that intensify your emotional spending. For example, do you tend to shop when you're with certain friends or in particular stores? Describe what's true for you.

_____

_____

_____

_____.

Reflection questions:

Now that you have identified your emotional spending triggers, take a moment to reflect on your findings. What insights did you gain from this exercise?

_____

_____.

How do these triggers contribute to your debt?

_____

_____.

Moving forward, how can you become more mindful of your emotional triggers and develop healthier coping mechanisms that don't involve spending money?

_____

_____.

How might your life change if you were able to break free from emotional spending and redirect those resources toward debt repayment or savings?

_____

_____.

What steps can you take to cultivate self-worth and self-esteem independent of material possessions?

_____

_____.

Understanding the emotions that drive your spending habits is a crucial step in addressing and overcoming emotional spending. Consider specific strategies or practices that can help you break free from the cycle of emotional spending. Remember, self-awareness and conscious decision-making are key to overcoming emotional spending. By recognizing your triggers, exploring healthier coping strategies, and developing mindful spending habits, you can gain control over your finances and work toward a debt-free life.

Activity: Reflecting on Shame and Debt

Take a moment to reflect on your personal experiences with shame and debt. Find a quiet space where you can focus and have a pen and paper or a digital device to jot down your thoughts.

Have you ever felt shame or embarrassment regarding your debt? How has it impacted your emotions, self-esteem, and relationships?

_____

_____

_____.

Are there specific situations or relationships in which you find it challenging to set healthy boundaries around lending money or managing your finances? How does this contribute to your debt or financial struggles?

_____

_____

_____.

Consider any societal or cultural pressures that may contribute to your feelings of shame about your financial situation. Are there any expectations or judgments from others that you internalize? For instance, are the clothes you wear or the car you drive a reflection of what *you* want—or what *others* expect? Do your purchases drive you into debt? Answer below.

_____

_____

_____.

Reflect on how shame or embarrassment may hinder your ability to seek help or talk openly about your debt. Are there any barriers preventing you from discussing your financial challenges with a therapist, friend, or family member?

_____

_____

_____.

The point here is to get you to see that you don't have to be ashamed about any facet of your personal finances, including having debt. The goal is simply to unburden yourself of the emotional worries, financial pressures, and associated toll of being in debt so that you can live a more care-free, fulfilled life.

Reducing Your Credit Card Balances

Paying off credit card debt and keeping balances low offers numerous benefits for your financial well-being. By reducing debt, you gain financial freedom and experience reduced stress. Your improved creditworthiness opens doors to better interest rates, increased access to credit, and improved financial opportunities. Moreover, maintaining low balances on credit accounts allows you to better manage your finances and build a solid foundation for your future financial goals. When it comes to achieving low credit card balances, there are several strategies to consider and tactics to get on the right path.

One key area to focus on is your credit card usage. Limit your credit card usage to essential expenses and aim to keep your balances low. High credit utilization ratios can negatively impact your credit score, so strive to keep your credit card balances below 30% of your available credit limit. By doing so, you showcase responsible financial behavior and avoid excessive interest charges.

The Five-step Credit Card Debt Repayment Plan

Now it's time to create your own credit card debt repayment plan. Follow five core steps and march on toward slaying your debt!

STEP 1: Assess Your Credit Card Debt

Make a list of all your credit card debts, including the balance, interest rate, and minimum payment for each. Calculate the total amount of debt you owe across all your credit cards. You can't craft a realistic payoff plan if you're in the dark about precisely how much you're in debt.

If it's hard for you to do this step, try motivating yourself by considering how your debt is affecting your financial well-being and daily life. Reflect on the emotions and stress associated with it. Then think of how great it'll feel to be rid of your debts.

STEP 2: Choose a Repayment Strategy

Determine if there are specific credit cards or debt factors that bother you the most. Identify your "area of pain" to prioritize your repayment strategy accordingly. In prioritizing the debt you most want to knock out, ask yourself: is it high interest rate debt that's bothering you, having high balances on your credit cards, or simply having too many credit cards, period? If you focus on what ails you most, you're more likely to remain motivated and stick to a debt payoff strategy.

Evaluate the debt snowball and debt avalanche methods too. The snowball method involves paying off the smallest debts first, while the avalanche method prioritizes debts with the highest interest rates. Which one aligns best with your financial situation and motivates you the most?

STEP 3: Set Your Repayment Goals

Define your long-term goal of becoming debt-free and establish a realistic timeline. Break down your total debt into smaller, manageable milestones or goals to track your progress along the way. Determine how much extra you can allocate toward debt repayment each month, and then implement your repayment plan.

STEP 4: Pay More Than the Minimum

Whenever possible, pay more than the minimum payment on your credit cards. Even small increments can make a difference. If you can, consider making additional payments whenever you have windfalls or unexpected income. If balance transfer or debt consolidation seems viable, explore those options and calculate potential savings in interest.

STEP 5: Seek Professional Guidance If Needed

If you feel overwhelmed or unsure about managing your credit card debt on your own, reach out to a credit counseling agency or financial advisor. Seek their advice on negotiating lower interest rates, creating a debt management plan, or exploring alternative options.

Reflection questions:

Take a moment to reflect on your current credit card debt situation and the steps you've outlined in your repayment plan. Consider the following questions:

How does your credit card debt impact your financial well-being and over-all stress levels?

_____

_____.

How would getting rid of credit card debt improve your life?

_____

_____.

What sacrifices or adjustments are you willing to make to allocate more funds toward debt repayment?

_____

_____.

How can you stay motivated throughout the process?

_____

_____.

Why did you get into debt in the first place? Was it one of the other Dreaded Ds or something else?

_____

_____.

What strategies can you implement to avoid accumulating additional credit card debt while you're currently trying to dig yourself out of debt?

_____

_____.

How can you develop healthier habits and avoid a burdensome level of
  debt in the future?

_____

_____.

Taking the First Step

Based on your reflections, what is the first action step you can take toward
implementing your credit card debt repayment plan? Is there anything you
need to research, organize, or initiate to get started? Write down what
you need to do and then make a commitment to yourself to do it!

_____

_____.

Final reflections:

How can you maintain a balance between repaying your debt and enjoying
  your life?

_____

_____.

What are some cost-effective alternatives to activities or purchases that
  may contribute to more debt?

_____

_____.

How can you build a support system to keep you accountable and motivated
  throughout your debt repayment journey? Are there friends, family, or
  online communities you can connect with?

_____

_____.

What financial goals do you have beyond debt repayment? How can you
  align your actions and savings with these goals to create a brighter
  financial future?

_____

_____.

Remember, breaking free from credit card debt takes time and persistence. Celebrate each milestone and maintain a positive mindset. With each payment, you're one step closer to financial freedom.

Evaluating Your Mortgage

Take a moment to evaluate your current mortgage situation and explore whether it's truly affordable—or a source of stress and financial challenge that you need to address. Answer a few questions to get a snapshot of your home affordability.

Do you struggle at all to make your monthly mortgage payment?   YES NO

Do you lack sufficient insurance coverage due to high costs?   YES NO

Do you find it difficult to pay your annual property taxes?   YES NO

Do you ever have sleepless nights about paying for your home?   YES NO

Do you pay more than 30% of your income for your residence?   YES NO

Do you find it challenging to pay utilities for your property? YES NO

Do you have deferred maintenance issues due to repair costs? YES NO

If you answered yes to *any* of the questions above, that's a red flag and a sign that you may need to lower your housing costs. If home affordability is an issue, research and make a list of potential options for managing your mortgage. This could include loan modification, refinancing, government programs, selling your home, or other alternatives. Write down the pros and cons of each option. Also, evaluate your eligibility for each option. Consider factors such as your credit score, income, employment status, and the requirements set by lenders or government programs.

Think about the potential impact of each option on your financial future. How would they affect your monthly payments, interest rates, or overall debt burden? Consider both short-term relief and long-term consequences.

Reflection questions:

How can you overcome any shame or embarrassment associated with exploring mortgage or alternative housing options?

_____

_____.

Who can you reach out to for support or guidance during this process?

_____

_____.

Assessing and Managing Your Auto Loan Debt

To effectively manage your auto loan debt, it's important to assess your current situation and explore strategies that can help you reduce the burden. Follow these steps to take control of your auto loan debt.

Evaluate Your Auto Loan

Review your loan terms, including the interest rate, monthly payments, and remaining balance.

Determine if you are upside down on your loan, meaning you owe more than the car is currently worth. Calculate the total cost of the loan, including interest, over the life of the loan.

Consider Refinancing

Research and compare loan options from different lenders to see if refinancing could lower your interest rate or extend the loan term. Calculate how refinancing would impact your monthly payments and the total cost of the loan.

Explore Selling or Trading Your Car

Assess the current market value of your car by researching similar models and their prices.

Determine if selling your car and using the proceeds to pay off the loan is a viable option.

If you're upside down on your loan, calculate the difference between the car's value and the loan balance, and consider how you can bridge that gap.

Evaluate Leasing as an Alternative

Research the pros and cons of leasing a car, including the lower monthly payments and potential restrictions. Assess if leasing aligns with your financial goals and long-term needs.

Seek Professional Assistance If Needed

Reach out to credit counseling agencies or financial advisors who can provide guidance on managing your auto loan debt. Discuss your options with them and explore potential negotiations with your lender.

Activity: Add It All Up

Many people are shocked when they see the true cost of car ownership. It's not only car payments, gas, and insurance. Having a vehicle requires a host of ongoing expenses. Use the following worksheet below to add up how much your set of wheels are really costing you.

Worksheet: My True Car Costs

Car payments: If you financed your vehicle through a loan and haven't yet paid off that note, you have monthly car payments to make, including the principal amount and interest.

Monthly amount: _____; yearly amount: _____

Depreciation: Cars depreciate over time, which means their value decreases. This is an important factor to consider if you plan to sell or trade in your vehicle in the future. Edmunds has an online tool to show you the true cost of owning a car, including depreciation for your vehicle. Find your depreciation amount by visiting: https://www.edmunds.com/tco.html.

Monthly amount: _____; yearly amount: _____

Insurance: Car insurance is a legal requirement in most places. The cost varies based on factors such as your age, driving history, location, and the type of coverage you choose.

Monthly amount: _____; yearly amount: _____

Fuel: The cost of gasoline or diesel fuel is an ongoing expense. Fuel prices can fluctuate based on market conditions and can vary depending on your location and the efficiency of your vehicle.

Monthly amount: _____; yearly amount: _____

Maintenance and repairs: Regular maintenance, such as oil changes, tire rotations, and brake inspections, is necessary to keep your car in good working condition. Additionally, unexpected repairs can arise, ranging from minor fixes to major component replacements.

Monthly amount: _____; yearly amount: _____

Vehicle registration and taxes: You'll need to register your car with the appropriate government agency and pay registration fees. Depending on where you live, there may also be annual or periodic taxes associated with car ownership.

Parking: If you don't have access to free parking, you may need to pay for parking spaces, whether it's at home, work, or in public areas. This cost can add up, especially in urban areas where parking fees are higher.

Monthly amount: _____; yearly amount: _____

Tolls: If you frequently use toll roads or bridges, you'll need to budget for the toll charges.

Monthly amount: _____; yearly amount: _____

Licensing and permits: Some regions require special licenses or permits for certain types of vehicles, such as motorcycles or commercial vehicles. These licenses and permits may involve additional fees.

Monthly amount: _____; yearly amount: _____

Roadside assistance: Joining a roadside assistance program can provide peace of mind in case of emergencies such as flat tires, breakdowns, or lockouts. However, it comes with an annual or monthly fee.

Monthly amount: _____; yearly amount: _____

Additional accessories: Personalizing your car with accessories such as floor mats, seat covers, or entertainment systems may come with extra costs.

Monthly amount: _____; yearly amount: _____

Cleaning and detailing: Regular cleaning and detailing keep your vehicle looking its best. This may involve car washes, detailing services, or buying cleaning supplies.

Monthly amount: _____; yearly amount: _____

Total monthly amount: _____; **total yearly amount:** _____

Were you surprised by how much your car actually costs? According to AAA's annual Your Driving Costs study, it costs $10,728—or $894 a month!—to own and operate the average new vehicle in America. How do your car costs stack up to those figures? It's important to note that the specific costs can vary depending on factors such as the type of car, your location, and your personal circumstances.

If you're looking to buy another car and want to fully understand your vehicle expenses, AAA has a new online Your Driving Costs calculator (at aaa.com/autorepair/drivingcosts), which gives car shoppers an interactive and personalized breakdown for different vehicles. This online tool lets you do a comprehensive cost analysis of a specific vehicle by category to determine what vehicle will best suit your budget. The data is available for new and used vehicles (going back five years). You can also customize your results based on your location and your own driving tendencies. Considering these expenses will help you budget effectively and make informed decisions about car ownership.

Reflection questions:

What does the car you drive say, if anything, about you?

_____
_____.

Is your car a status symbol for you? Why or why not?

_____
_____.

Which strategies, such as refinancing, selling, or leasing, resonate with you the most? Why do you believe the chosen strategies would be best or most cost-effective in your situation?

_____
_____.

Developing a Student Loan Repayment Strategy

To effectively manage and eliminate your college debt, it's important to develop a repayment strategy tailored to your specific situation. Use the following 10-step plan to create a strategy for tackling your student loans.

Step 1. Understand Your Loan Types and Loan Servicers

Identify all your student loans, including federal and private loans. Also, find out who is the loan servicing company for each college loan you owe.

Step 2: Get the Details on All Loans

Determine the interest rates, loan balances, and repayment terms for each loan you owe.

Step 3: Calculate the Total Amount of Student Loan Debt You Owe

It might not be pretty when you add it all up. There may be far more interest than anticipated, or those periods of deferment or forbearance may have added extra costs to your loans. But clarity about what you owe is crucial. Once you know where things stand, your finances aren't often as scary as you may have thought.

Step 4: Research Repayment Options

Understand the various repayment plans available for federal loans, such as standard, graduated, extended, and income-driven plans.

Step 5: Pick Your Optimal Repayment Plan

Evaluate which repayment plan aligns best with your financial circumstances and long-term goals.

Step 6: Examine Forgiveness Options

Consider the potential benefits of federal loan forgiveness programs, such as Public Service Loan Forgiveness (PSLF) or targeted forgiveness programs for specific professions. Despite the Supreme Court saying in 2023 that President Joe Biden's plan to cancel student loan debt was unconstitutional, the Biden administration has offered several other ways to get student loan relief. Conduct an Internet search to review the latest details on these ongoing and evolving efforts.

Step 7: Explore Refinancing and Consolidation

Assess whether refinancing your student loans with a private lender can provide lower interest rates or more favorable repayment terms. Understand the potential trade-offs of refinancing, such as losing access to federal loan benefits. Determine if consolidating your federal loans into a Direct Consolidation Loan is a viable option (or even necessary) to simplify payments.

Step 8: Research Employer Assistance Programs

Inquire about employer-sponsored student loan repayment assistance programs available at your current or potential future employers. Understand the eligibility criteria, payment terms, and any obligations associated with these programs. You typically have to agree to work for an employer for a given time period in order to gain this benefit. Evaluate how participation in such programs can accelerate your repayment progress.

Step 9: Explore Loan Forgiveness Programs

Determine if you qualify for federal loan forgiveness programs, such as PSLF, Teacher Loan Forgiveness, or forgiveness programs for specific professions. Understand the requirements, service obligations, and documentation needed to qualify for loan forgiveness. Consider, too, if pursuing a career in public service or targeted professions aligns with your goals and loan forgiveness opportunities.

Step 10: Seek Professional Guidance If Needed

If you're overwhelmed with the process or just can't get a handle on your college debt, consult with a student loan counselor or financial advisor who specializes in student loan debt.

Discuss your repayment options, loan forgiveness opportunities, and employer assistance programs to receive personalized advice. Seek assistance in preparing and submitting applications for loan forgiveness or employer-sponsored programs.

Reflection questions:

Take a few moments to reflect on your student loan debt, consider the following questions, and write about how college loans have impacted your life and your finances.

Looking back, was it worth it for you to take out student loans? Why or why not?

_____

_____

_____

_____.

How do your student loans impact you overall?

_____

_____.

Have your student loans prevented you from achieving any goals?

_____

_____.

Which repayment options, such as income-driven plans, refinancing, or loan forgiveness programs, align with your financial circumstances and long-term goals? Why do you believe these strategies would be effective for your situation?

_____

_____.

Based on your reflections, what is the first action step you can take toward better managing and eliminating your student loan debt? Is there any research, calculation, or communication with lenders or employers that you need to initiate? If so, write it down below.

The very first step I can take to better manage my student loans is:

Step 1: _____.

I can also take the following steps to reduce my college debt:

Step 2: _____

Step 3: _____.

None of us can snap our fingers and make student loan debt magically disappear. But there are ways to chip away at it and make college loans less of a factor in your life. Stay focused on your goals and appreciate the progress you make along the way. By actively managing this obligation, and exploring available options, you're taking control of your finances and setting yourself up for a brighter future.

Creating a Plan to Resolve Tax Debt

Resolving tax debt requires careful planning and action. Follow these steps to create a plan that will help you manage and eliminate your tax debt:

Assess Your Tax Debt

Determine the total amount of tax debt you owe, including any penalties and interest.

Review your tax returns and supporting documents to ensure the accuracy of the debt.

Understand Your Repayment Options

Research the different payment plans offered by the IRS, such as short-term and long-term installment agreements. Determine which payment plan is best suited to your financial situation and ability to make monthly payments. Consider the eligibility criteria, fees, and requirements associated with each payment plan option.

Apply for an Installment Agreement

Determine if you qualify for an online payment agreement based on the IRS requirements.

Use the IRS Online Payment Agreement tool to apply for a payment plan, or alternatively, submit Form 9465, Installment Agreement Request, by mail. Follow the instructions provided by the IRS and provide accurate and complete information.

Explore an Offer in Compromise

Determine if you meet the eligibility criteria for an offer in compromise. Consult with a tax professional or attorney to assess your chances of success and guide you through the process.

Prepare and submit the necessary documentation and forms to the IRS, including Form 656, Offer in Compromise.

Consider Innocent Spouse Relief

If necessary, determine if you qualify for innocent spouse relief based on the IRS guidelines.

Prepare and submit to the IRS Form 8857, Request for Innocent Spouse Relief, along with supporting documents. Consult with a tax professional or attorney to evaluate your eligibility and guide you through the application process.

Seek Professional Assistance

Consult with a tax professional or attorney who specializes in tax debt resolution.

Provide them with all relevant documentation and information related to your tax debt.

Follow their guidance and instructions throughout the process, including negotiations with the IRS.

Maintain Open Communication with the IRS

Don't make the mistake of panicking about your tax issues and sticking your head in the sand. Respond promptly to any correspondence or requests from the IRS. Keep detailed records of all communications, including dates, names of IRS representatives, and copies of correspondence.

Notify the IRS of any changes in your financial circumstances that may impact your ability to meet your payment obligations.

Stay Committed to Your Repayment Plan

Make regular, on-time payments according to the terms of your installment agreement.

Adjust your budget and expenses to ensure you can meet your monthly payment obligations.

Continuously monitor your progress and reassess your financial situation periodically.

Reflection questions:

Dealing with the Tax Man worries a lot of people. Take some time to reflect on your tax debt situation, the emotional and financial impact, as well as the steps you've outlined for resolving it. Consider the following questions:

How has your tax debt affected your financial well-being and overall stress levels?

_____

_____.

What positive changes do you anticipate once you've resolved your tax debt?

_____

_____.

Which repayment option (installment agreement, offer in compromise, innocent spouse relief) do you believe is most suitable for your situation? Why have you chosen this approach?

_____

_____.

What challenges or obstacles do you anticipate while implementing your tax debt resolution plan? How can you overcome these challenges and stay committed to your goals?

_____

_____.

Based on your reflection, what is the first action step you can take toward resolving your tax debt? Is there any research, consultation with professionals, or communication with the IRS that you need to initiate?

_____

_____.

How can you improve your tax compliance and record-keeping practices to avoid future tax debt? Are there resources or tools you can leverage to ensure accurate reporting and minimize potential errors?

_____

_____.

How will you adjust your financial management and budgeting practices to prevent a recurrence of tax debt? Are there habits or strategies you can adopt to maintain a healthy financial position?

_____

_____.

Resolving tax debt requires a willingness to tackle the problem head-on, knowledge of your options, and the right resources and support. By following your plan and seeking professional assistance when necessary, you're taking important steps toward freeing yourself from the burden of tax debt and achieving financial stability.

The journey to becoming debt-free is a transformative process that goes beyond the numbers on your balance sheet. It's about regaining control of your financial life, learning from past mistakes, and building a solid foundation for a brighter future. You don't have to be ashamed about any debt problems you have. Debt is a widespread issue that affects people from all walks of life. Many Americans find themselves burdened by various forms of debt, such as mortgages, student loans, credit card debt, and more. And I know from firsthand experience that the weight of debt can be overwhelming, limiting financial freedom and hindering progress toward important goals.

However, debt doesn't have to become a way of life. Being debt-free is not only possible but within your reach. You can use practical strategies, support, and the right approach to tackle different types of debt, empower yourself, and reclaim your financial life. You won't travel the exact path that I did, as the journey to debt freedom is a personal one, and everyone's path may look different. But stay focused, remain resilient, and celebrate each milestone along the way. You have the power to shape your financial future and create a life that is free from the burden of debt.

As we conclude this ninth chapter of _The Bounce Back Workbook_, which focused on debt, take time to think about what you have just done, felt, and discovered. What emotions surfaced for you during the exercises? What lessons have you learned so far, and what growth have you experienced? Write a recap below.

_____

_____

_____

_____

_____

Chapter 10

Damaged Credit

B ad credit. It's a term that can put a knot in the pit of your stomach if you know what it's like to have a poor credit rating. A low credit score can follow you around like a shadow, impacting every facet of your life. It hurts your chances of renting an apartment or getting a mortgage. It impacts your ability to get certain jobs, since lots of employers perform credit checks. And of course, a less-than-stellar credit profile drives up the cost of borrowing on everything from mortgages and credit cards to college loans and personal loans.

But here's the good news: You can recover from bad credit. This section of *The Bounce Back Workbook* is about understanding the impacts of bad credit, both emotional and financial, and providing you with a game plan to overcome your credit setbacks and achieve your own financial success. In this chapter, we'll explore the difficulties and consequences of damaged credit and highlight valuable strategies and support to repair and rebuild your creditworthiness. Whether you have experienced financial stumbles, defaulted on payments, or faced other circumstances that have negatively impacted your credit, my goal is to assist you in regaining control of your credit and making credit worries a thing of the past.

Reflecting on Your Credit Journey

Speaking of the past, take a moment to look back on your own credit journey over the years. Consider the following questions:

How has your credit impacted your life over time? What challenges, if any, have you faced?

_____

_____.

How do you feel when you think about your credit score? What emotions arise?

_____

_____.

Have you ever been denied anything or had to pay a higher price due to your credit rating?

_____

_____.

What would it mean to you to overcome any credit issues and have perfect credit?

_____

_____.

Personal Storytelling Activity: Share Your Credit Story

Describe your experiences and how your credit has affected your finances, life, or relationships.

_____

_____

_____

_____.

Now consider also sharing your story with a trusted friend or in a support group. Such sharing can be cathartic and can help you gain support and perspective. By openly discussing your history or current struggles, you also take away the weight of isolation and secrecy about your credit, which can reduce any shame you may feel.

Understanding Your Credit Reports

Obtain a free copy of your credit report from each of the three major credit reporting agencies (Equifax, TransUnion, and Experian) through AnnualCreditReport.com. Federal law gives you your reports from each bureau once a year free of charge. Review your credit reports carefully, considering the following:

- Are there any errors or inaccuracies in your personal information, credit accounts, inquiries, public records, or collections accounts?
- Do you recognize all the accounts listed on your credit reports?
- Are there any discrepancies between the credit reports from different agencies?

Identifying Errors and Disputing Inaccurate Information

Identify any errors or inaccuracies in your credit reports. If you find any, write a letter of dispute to the credit reporting agencies, explaining the errors and providing any supporting documentation. Take note of the steps you need to follow to initiate a dispute. All three credit bureaus offer you a way to dispute credit information online at their websites.

Understanding Credit Scores and the Causes of a Poor Credit Rating

Your FICO credit score is calculated based on a variety of factors, including payment history (35%), credit utilization (30%), length of credit history (15%), credit mix (10%), and new credit or inquiries (10%). Payment history refers to your track record of making on-time payments for loans and credit cards, which is the most significant factor in determining your credit score. Credit utilization measures the amount of credit you're currently using compared to your total available credit, and maintaining a low utilization rate is generally favorable for your score. The length of your credit history considers how long you've been using credit, with longer histories often seen as more favorable. Credit mix evaluates the types of credit you have, such as credit cards, mortgages, or student loans, and having a diverse mix can positively impact your score. Finally, new credit or inquiries examines recent applications for credit, as multiple inquiries within a short period may suggest a higher risk.

By understanding these components, you can take steps to improve your credit score over time, such as making timely payments, keeping credit utilization low, and maintaining a healthy mix of credit types. Of course, the *opposite* of doing these things means you'll *lower* your credit score. So whenever you have to do any financial transactions that are credit-related, keep these five credit-scoring factors in mind.

Systemic and Structural Issues That Contribute to Poor Credit

African American, Hispanic, or Asian people in America have generally had lower credit scores than white Americans. For example, Black people have the lowest credit scores of all populations—a trend that has, sadly, been the case for many decades. This isn't the case, however, of Black people just being financially irresponsible. Historically and from a contemporary standpoint, systemic discrimination and racism have contributed to the lower credit scores often seen among Black people and other minority groups in comparison to white Americans.

The effects of centuries-long racial inequality, discriminatory practices, and limited access to economic opportunities have created significant disparities in wealth accumulation, employment, and education. These disparities directly impact creditworthiness and credit access. Discrimination in housing, employment, and lending practices has restricted the ability of people of color to build credit histories and access affordable credit. Limited access to quality education and job opportunities, coupled with income disparities, can result in lower financial literacy levels and a higher likelihood of financial hardships, including difficulties in making timely payments on loans and credit cards.

Furthermore, the lack of generational wealth, which is often a result of past discriminatory policies, hinders many communities of color in their ability to access favorable loan terms and establish a solid credit foundation. Addressing these systemic issues and promoting equitable access to economic resources and opportunities are crucial steps toward reducing the racial credit score gap and fostering a more just and inclusive financial system.

Black people aren't the only marginalized individuals that bear the brunt of discriminatory practices that wind up affecting people's credit. A study from the Center for LGBTQ Economic Advancement and Research found that LGBTQ Americans were twice as likely to have "poor" or "very poor" credit scores as non-LGBTQ respondents. Additionally, same-sex couples are 73% more likely to be denied mortgages.

Activity: Identifying the Causes of Your Bad Credit

Even as we acknowledge systemic issues that affect a person's credit and overall finances, it's important to also evaluate our personal behaviors. Reflect on the factors that have contributed to your bad credit. Consider the following:

- Have you made late payments or missed payments on your credit accounts?
- Have you maxed out your credit cards or used a high percentage of your available credit?
- Have you defaulted on loans or faced collections accounts?
- Have you experienced discrimination or bias that affected your ability to manage your credit?
- Which factors do you think have the most significant impact on your credit score and why?
- Have you experienced any legal judgments or bankruptcies that have impacted your credit score?
- How many credit inquiries have you had in the past two years? Have you been mindful of applying for credit only when necessary?
- Do you have a good mix of credit or mostly just one form of credit?

Activity: Taking Responsibility for Your Credit Situation

Take responsibility for your credit situation by acknowledging the factors within your control that have led to your bad credit. Write a letter to yourself, accepting responsibility for your own actions and committing to making positive changes.

_____

_____

_____

_____

_____.

Reflection questions:

How does accepting responsibility for your credit situation empower you to make necessary changes? How can you learn from past mistakes to create a better financial future?

_____

_____

_____

_____.

In the next sections of this chapter, we will explore strategies to improve your credit, such as piggybacking, using secured credit cards, and adding nontraditional payments to your credit reports. Along the way, you glean the necessary insights for achieving excellent credit and the right mindset required for credit recovery.

Activity: Setting Credit Improvement Goals

Based on your reflection, set specific credit improvement goals for each credit score factor. For example, if your credit utilization ratio is high, aim to reduce it to below 30%. Write down your goals and create a plan to achieve them.

Credit factor: payment history. My goal is: _____

_____

Credit factor: debt/credit usage. My goal is: _____

_____

Credit factor: length of credit. My goal is: _____

_____

Credit factor: mix of credit. My goal is: _____

_____

Credit factor: inquiries. My goal is: _____

_____

Piggybacking Your Way to a Higher Credit Score

Are there any individuals in your life with good credit who might be willing to add you as an authorized user on their credit card? If so, you should consider the potential benefits (and the possible drawbacks) of piggybacking as a credit maneuver. Piggybacking is when an individual becomes an authorized user on someone else's credit card account in order to benefit from their positive credit history. This strategy can be especially useful for individuals who have limited or poor credit history and are looking to boost their credit scores.

If there are people in your life with good credit who are willing to add you as an authorized user, it can potentially have several benefits. First their positive payment history and responsible credit behavior can be reflected on your credit report, which may help improve your credit score. Additionally, being associated with a credit card that has a long-standing history and low credit utilization can positively impact your credit profile. This strategy can provide you with an opportunity to establish a credit foundation or rebuild your credit if you have faced challenges in the past.

However, it is important to consider possible drawbacks as well. If the primary cardholder fails to make timely payments or mismanages their credit, it could negatively affect your credit score. Similarly, if they carry high levels of debt or utilize a large portion of their available credit, it could potentially harm your credit utilization ratio. Therefore, before pursuing piggybacking, it is essential to have open and honest discussions with the primary cardholder, set clear expectations, and ensure that they maintain responsible credit habits too.

Make a list of three family members you think might have good to excellent credit. Approach them and inquire directly (but tactfully) about their credit ratings or credit scores. Don't assume! With relatives who do, indeed, have great credit, consider asking them about adding you as an authorized user on one of their cards. Let them know that you don't even have to get the card. When it comes it the mail, they can simply put it in their wallet, or stash it in a drawer for safekeeping.

Family member #1: _____

Family member #2: _____

Family member #3: _____

Secured Credit Cards

Getting a secured credit card is another way to boost your credit score and strengthen your credit rating. A secured credit card is a type of credit card that requires a cash deposit as collateral. The deposit acts as security for the credit card issuer, reducing the risk associated with lending to individuals with limited or poor credit histories. The amount of the deposit typically determines the credit limit on the secured card. By using a secured credit card responsibly and making timely payments, you can demonstrate your creditworthiness and build a positive credit history.

One of the benefits of a secured credit card is that it allows you to establish or rebuild your credit even if you have been denied traditional unsecured credit cards in the past. As you consistently make on-time payments and keep your credit utilization low, your credit score can gradually improve over time. Another benefit is that you really can't overspend in the way that you can with a regular unsecured credit card. If you don't have the money on deposit in the account, your secured card transaction won't go through. So it forces you to only spend what you have. Additionally, some secured credit card issuers may periodically review your account and offer opportunities to upgrade to an unsecured credit card once you have demonstrated responsible credit behavior.

It is important to note that not all secured credit cards are the same, and terms and conditions can vary. Before applying for a secured credit card, it is advisable to research different options, compare fees and interest rates, and choose one that best fits your financial needs. With responsible use, a secured credit card can serve as a valuable tool in building credit and achieving your long-term financial goals. If you opt for a secured credit card, the most important thing is to research and confirm that they report your payment history to all three major credit bureaus. After doing your homework, make a list of three potential secured credit cards that align with your needs.

Secured credit card option #1: _____

Secured credit card option #2: _____

Secured credit card option #3: _____

TEST YOUR KNOWLEDGE

What are three benefits to piggybacking off someone else's credit?

Benefit #1: _____

Benefit #2: _____

Benefit #3: _____

What is one potential drawback to piggybacking off another person's credit?

_____

What are two benefits of using secured cards?

Benefit #1: _____

Benefit #2: _____

Exploring Rent and Nontraditional Payments Reporting

You can also build up your credit by adding rent and nontraditional payments to your credit files. In recent years, rent reporting has become recognized as a widely accepted way to determine people's creditworthiness. After all, rent is often the biggest expense for individuals, and including it in credit files provides a more comprehensive view of their financial responsibility.

Rent reporting services allow you to report your rental payments to credit bureaus, which then incorporate this data into your credit history. By consistently making on-time rent payments, you can establish a positive payment history and potentially boost your credit score. This is particularly beneficial if you have a limited credit history, or you prefer to build your credit without going into debt.

In addition to rent, some nontraditional payments, such as utility bills, telecommunications bills, and even subscription services, can now be reported to credit bureaus as well. These nontraditional payments, when reported and consistently paid on time, can help diversify your credit profile and demonstrate your ability to manage various financial obligations.

However, it's important to note that not all landlords or service providers participate in rent reporting or nontraditional payment reporting. Before relying on these methods, confirm with your landlord or service providers if they report payments to credit bureaus or consider using third-party services that specialize in reporting such payments. Research the rent reporting services mentioned in *Bounce Back* (services such as Rental Kharma, Esusu, RentReporters, PayYourRent, and Jetty Credit). Compare their features, fees, and the credit bureaus to whom they report. By leveraging rent and nontraditional payment reporting, you can strengthen your credit history and improve your creditworthiness in a more comprehensive manner.

Reflection questions:

How will you ensure consistent and timely payments for rent and nontraditional bills? What strategies or systems will you put in place to avoid late or missed payments?

_____

_____.

How will you keep thorough documentation of your rent and nontraditional payments? Will you use digital tools, such as scanning receipts and statements, or maintain physical copies?

_____

_____.

What are your expectations for the impact of rent reporting on your creditworthiness? How will you measure and track your progress?

_____

_____.

Think about your credit history and the challenges you may have faced. Consider your aspirations for your credit future. Now, imagine yourself with a perfect credit rating. How would that impact your life? What doors would it open for you? How would it make you feel? Visualize the benefits and opportunities that come with perfect credit.

As we conclude this tenth chapter of *The Bounce Back Workbook*, which focused on damaged credit, take time to think about what you have just done, felt, and discovered. What emotions surfaced for you during the exercises? What lessons have you learned so far, and what growth have you experienced? Write a recap below.

_____

_____

_____

_____

_____

Chapter 11

Dollar Deficits

L iving with dollar deficits, where your income is barely sufficient to cover your expenses and savings seem out of reach, can be incredibly stressful and limiting. In this chapter of *The Bounce Back Workbook*, we'll address the underlying factors that contribute to dollar deficits and walk through practical steps to improve your financial circumstances, increase your savings, and build a strong financial future. Whether you are struggling to make ends meet, constantly worried about money, or looking to improve your retirement security, this chapter is designed to empower you to take control of your finances and achieve lasting economic stability.

Activity: Breathe and Prepare

Pause for a moment to simply take a deep breath. I realize that when you're overwhelmed or stressed about money issues, it's hard to even know where to begin. So just relax for a moment and slow down your breathing. Go find a quiet space, then close your eyes for a minute, and just inhale and exhale deeply. Once you're ready, then you can begin to prepare to focus, reflect on any dollar deficits you may be facing, and document your thoughts and actions accordingly.

Think now about your own financial circumstances and any challenges you may be experiencing, such as living paycheck to paycheck, having little to no savings, or struggling to pay your bills.

Maybe you're actually not in the midst of dollar deficits, but you're really just looking to save more money, better invest and plan for the future, or take your finances to the next level. Whatever your unique circumstances, now is the time to imagine a future where you have achieved the financial stability and prosperity you desire and deserve.

Reflection questions:

How would complete financial security change your life? What opportunities would it open up for you? How would it make you feel?

_____

_____

_____.

Whatever your current circumstances, whether good or bad, how did you get here? Describe whatever you feel has led up to your present financial condition.

_____

_____

_____

_____

_____

_____.

Saving Money and Budgeting

Almost everyone would love to save more money or have more cash in the bank. But not everybody likes to do one thing that helps with saving money, and that's budgeting. Consider how you've managed your finances in recent years, and think back on the highs and the lows.

Can you identify periods when you had savings or when you budgeted properly? If so, when were you feeling more flushed with cash, and what were the circumstances? If not, describe how long you've been battling dollar deficits. Has it been your whole life or a specific time period?

_____

_____

_____

_____.

There are three important strategies that will help you stretch your dollars and make the most of your current income, still live a happy life today without being overly restrictive, and still plan for the future. These strategies are: creating a realistic budget, developing required savings accounts, and making a financial plan B to prepare you for the unexpected. Let's look at each of these strategies and what's required.

And don't worry. Even if you've never been able to budget or save before, I'm going to share some tips and techniques with you that will help boost your confidence and affirm that you can indeed become a successful budgeter and saver starting now—and create the future security you want too.

Becoming a Better Budgeter: Mastering the Art of Financial Management

Budgeting is a fundamental skill for effective financial management. By following some straightforward steps and implementing four cardinal rules of budgeting, you can become a better budgeter and take control of your financial future.

Step 1: Prioritize Your Purchases

Start by distinguishing between your needs and wants. Create a list of items you *need* versus those you *want*. This will help you determine what you can afford and what you should save up for later. Avoid impulse purchases by shopping with a planned list, focusing on your necessities.

Step 2: Set Realistic Savings Goals

Evaluate your spending habits honestly. Determine how much you can realistically save each week by reevaluating discretionary expenses such as eating out or entertainment. Identify what you're willing to give up to reach your savings goals, striking a balance between cutting expenses and maintaining a satisfying lifestyle.

Step 3: Keep It Simple

Choose a budgeting method that works best for you, whether it's an Excel spreadsheet, online budgeting software, or pen and paper. Keep your budget straightforward and easily accessible so you can quickly reference it when making purchasing decisions or considering big-ticket items. Simplify your budgeting process to make it more manageable and sustainable.

Step 4: Include a Miscellaneous Category

Allocate a portion of your budget for unexpected small expenses that may arise during the week. This miscellaneous category covers items such as last-minute grocery needs, additional gas expenses, or forgotten snacks. By accounting for these unplanned expenses, you maintain flexibility in your budget while staying on track. Neglecting to include this category can lead to budget deviations caused by accumulated small expenses.

Step 5: Track Your Spending

Develop the habit of tracking your purchases and expenditures in real time. Avoid waiting until the end of the week or month to review your spending. By tracking expenses as you make them, you increase awareness of your spending habits and may naturally reduce unnecessary expenses.

Step 6: Adopt a Cash-only Mindset

Break the habit of relying on credit cards and commit to spending only the money you have. Avoid using credit cards for purchases or bill payments until you have full control over your budget. Your budget should encompass all living and entertainment expenses while remaining flexible enough to accommodate unexpected expenditures. Relying on credit cards can lead to overspending beyond your monthly budget, making it crucial to resist this financial temptation.

Now, let's dive into the four essential rules of budgeting that will significantly impact your financial management.

Rule 1: Avoid Overspending

The cardinal rule of budgeting is simple but often overlooked: you cannot spend more than you earn. Living beyond your means leads to deficit spending, regardless of your income level. Assess your expenses, compare them to your net income (take-home pay), and cut out luxuries and nonessential purchases to align your spending with your income.

Rule 2: Add 20% to Your Planned Expenses

To ensure that you account for all monthly expenses, implement the 20% rule. Add 20% to the bottom-line number of your monthly expenses to accommodate overlooked categories and one-time expenses. This cushion provides flexibility in case of unexpected expenses or fluctuations in spending. If you don't spend the extra 20%, consider using it to pay down debts or boost your savings.

Rule 3: Reward Yourself with Treats Along the Way

To maintain long-term budget adherence, incorporate planned treats or rewards into your financial plan. Choose rewards that bring you joy and motivate you to stick to your budget. Allocate a monthly budget for expenses related to a hobby or interest, ensuring they are modest yet meaningful and won't lead to regretful spending.

Rule 4: Include a Savings Category in Your Budget

Don't overlook the importance of savings. Add a "Savings" category to your budget, regardless of the amount you can save. Even a small contribution helps build financial security and prepares you for unexpected expenses without derailing your budget. Regularly setting aside savings is crucial for long-term financial stability.

By following these six steps and integrating the four rules of budgeting into your financial practices, you'll become a better budgeter. Take control of your finances, avoid overspending, maintain a realistic budget, and reward yourself along the way. With dedication and discipline, you'll achieve your financial goals and secure a brighter future. The Budgeting Worksheet Below will help you get started.

Get Motivated to Budget with Your Money Board

Let's now go beyond the nuts and bolts of budgeting and do something more creative to make you *want* to budget and bring your dreams to reality. Try out this activity and have fun with it!

Title: My Money Vision Board
Objective: Create a visual representation of your financial aspirations, values, and goals through a money vision board.

Follow these instructions:

Step 1: Gather Supplies

Poster board or corkboard;

Magazines, newspapers, or printouts with images related to money, financial goals, and aspirations;

Scissors;

(Continued)

Glue or tape;

Markers or pens;

Any additional craft supplies (optional).

Step 2: Reflect on Your Financial Goals and Values

Take a moment to think about your financial goals, aspirations, and values. Consider questions such as:

What do you want to achieve financially?

What values guide your financial decisions?

How do you envision financial success for yourself, on your terms?

What are your long-term dreams and aspirations?

What would bring you joy and contentment?

Step 3: Collect Inspiring Images and Words

Go online or flip through magazines, newspapers, or printouts to find images, words, and phrases that resonate with your financial goals, values, and aspirations. Look for visuals that represent wealth, financial freedom, security, happiness, or any other themes that align with your vision.

Step 4: Create Your Money Vision Board

Start arranging the images, words, and phrases on your poster board or corkboard. Allow your creativity to flow as you create a visually appealing and meaningful composition. Consider the following tips:

Arrange the visuals in a way that tells a story or reflects a journey toward financial success.

Add personal touches such as handwritten quotes, affirmations, or goals using markers or pens.

Consider using colors, patterns, or other craft supplies to enhance your vision board.

Consider making elements of the vision board portray your unique personality, style, or vibe.

Step 5: Reflect on Your Money Vision Board

Once you've completed your vision board, take a step back and observe the overall composition. Reflect on the following questions:

What emotions or feelings arise when you look at your vision board?

_____

_____.

How does it align with your current financial reality?

_____

_____.

Are there any insights or surprises that come up for you? If so, what are they?

_____

_____.

Step 6: Display and Review Your Money Vision Board

Find a prominent place to display your vision board where you can see it regularly. Make it a habit to review your board and reconnect with your financial goals and aspirations. Consider scheduling regular check-ins to assess your progress and make adjustments to your financial plans as needed.

This activity allows you to visualize and connect with your financial goals on a deeper level. It serves as a visual reminder of what you're working toward and can provide inspiration and motivation throughout your financial journey. Enjoy the process of creating your money vision board and let it serve as a positive tool for shaping your financial future.

The Differences Between a Rainy Day Fund and an Emergency Fund

Differentiating between a rainy day fund and an emergency fund is also essential for effective financial planning. While both funds serve to address unforeseen expenses, they have distinct purposes and funding requirements.

A rainy day fund is designed to cover smaller, short-term expenses that may arise unexpectedly. These expenses could include car repairs, appliance replacements, or other similar incidents. Think of it as an umbrella you carry to shield yourself during a passing rain shower. Although you can't predict precisely when you'll need it, you know such situations are likely to occur. It is advisable to save at least a few hundred dollars in your rainy day fund, with some individuals opting for an extra safety net of up to $1,000.

On the other hand, an emergency fund serves a broader and more significant purpose. It is specifically reserved for financial emergencies that may have long-term effects, such as job loss, serious illnesses, or major unexpected expenses. Unlike the rainy day fund, which covers minor incidents, an emergency fund acts as a safety net for extended periods of financial hardship. To determine how much to save in your emergency fund, consider calculating your expenses for three to six months if you were to face unemployment or a major financial setback. This estimate will provide a rough guideline for the amount you should aim to save.

It's important to keep these funds separate to avoid confusion and ensure proper allocation of savings. By distinguishing between the two, you can withdraw funds from the appropriate fund without unintentionally depleting one when you actually need it. Maintaining separate accounts or clearly demarcating the funds within one account is crucial for effective management.

Ultimately, having both a rainy day fund and an emergency fund provides comprehensive financial protection. While the rainy day fund handles smaller unexpected expenses, the emergency fund safeguards against more significant financial setbacks. By maintaining both funds, you can confidently navigate unforeseen circumstances, regardless of their size or duration. Remember, it's all right to start with modest contributions and gradually build your funds over time. The key is to prioritize regular savings to ensure you're prepared for any financial situation that may arise.

Worksheet: Building Your Financial Safety Nets

Objective: Evaluate your current financial preparedness and create a plan to establish and maintain your rainy day and emergency funds.

Instructions:
Assess Your Current Financial Situation:

a. Calculate your monthly expenses, including bills, groceries, and other necessities.

b. Determine your average monthly income and any additional sources of income.

c. Evaluate your current savings and determine how much you have allocated to rainy day and emergency funds (if any).

Define Your Rainy Day Fund:

a. Identify potential short-term expenses that could arise unexpectedly (e.g. car repairs, appliance replacements, medical co-pays).

b. Determine the desired amount you would like to have in your rainy day fund, considering the range between a few hundred dollars to $1,000.

c. Assess your current savings and calculate how much you need to save to reach your rainy day fund goal.

Establish Your Rainy Day Fund:

a. Set a monthly savings target for your rainy day fund based on your budget and financial capacity.

b. Explore ways to cut expenses or increase income to allocate more toward your fund.

c. Determine a time frame for reaching your rainy day fund goal and mark milestones along the way.

Define Your Emergency Fund:

a. Evaluate potential long-term financial emergencies such as job loss, major medical expenses, or extended periods without income.

b. Calculate your monthly expenses and multiply by the number of months you would like your emergency fund to cover (e.g. 3–6 months).

c. Determine the desired amount you would like to have in your emergency fund to provide adequate protection during difficult times.

Establish Your Emergency Fund:

a. Set a monthly savings target for your emergency fund based on your budget and financial capacity.

b. Explore strategies to increase your savings rate, such as reducing discretionary spending or seeking additional income sources.

c. Create a timeline for reaching your emergency fund goal, and adjust your savings plan accordingly.

(Continued)

Monitor and Maintain:

a. Regularly review your progress toward your rainy day and emergency fund goals.
b. Adjust your savings plan as needed to stay on track or accommodate changing circumstances.
c. Continuously educate yourself on personal finance, investment options, and strategies for growing your safety nets.

Building your financial safety nets takes time and consistency. Be patient with the process, and just stick to your goals, and you will definitely see progress. Regularly reassess and update your funds as your financial situation evolves. By establishing and maintaining your rainy day and emergency funds, you'll gain peace of mind and greater financial security for the future.

Creating a Financial Plan B

To overcome dollar deficits and create a strong financial backup plan, it's important to anticipate potential scenarios and take proactive steps to mitigate risks. Some key strategies to implement include:

Assess your current financial situation: Take stock of your income, expenses, debts, and savings to understand where you stand.

Create reserve funds: Build both a rainy-day fund for smaller unexpected expenses and an emergency fund for larger, long-term disruptions. Save a portion of your income specifically for these purposes.

Develop a comprehensive budget: Track your expenses, prioritize your spending, and allocate funds to savings and future goals. Use the strategies mentioned earlier in the chapter to create a realistic and effective budget.

Protect yourself with insurance: Review your insurance coverage to ensure you have adequate protection for your home, car, health, and life. Insurance plays a crucial role in financial security.

Diversify your income: Explore additional income streams such as freelancing, part-time work, or starting a side business. Relying on a single source of income can be risky, so diversifying your income can provide more stability.

Educate yourself about personal finance: Learn about investing, retirement planning, and other financial strategies to secure your future. Knowledge is power when it comes to managing your finances effectively.

Seek professional advice: Consult with a financial advisor who can provide personalized guidance tailored to your specific needs and goals. They can help you develop a financial backup plan and provide insights into investment opportunities.

Reflection questions:

Imagine losing your job. What steps would you take to navigate this situation? How would you ensure a stable income?

_____

_____.

Visualize a major health expense. How would you cover the medical bills? What insurance coverage do you have in place?

_____

_____.

Think about a natural disaster damaging your home. What measures would you take to protect your property and ensure financial stability?

_____

_____.

Reflect on a significant drop in your income. How would you adjust your budget and expenses to accommodate the change?

_____

_____.

Envision a situation where you have to support yourself without a partner's income. What financial steps would you take to ensure your financial independence?

_____

_____.

Creating a financial backup plan is an ongoing process. Regularly reassess your plan, adapt to changing circumstances, and stay proactive in managing your finances. By taking these steps, you'll be better prepared to navigate any unexpected financial challenges that may arise and achieve economic security and success.

As we conclude this eleventh chapter of *The Bounce Back Workbook*, which focused on dollar deficits, take time to think about what you have just done, felt, and discovered. What emotions surfaced for you during the exercises? What lessons have you learned so far, and what growth have you experienced? Write a recap below.

_____

_____

_____

_____

_____

Chapter 12

Discrimination

Discrimination, in all its forms, has a profound impact on individuals, families, and society as a whole. It perpetuates inequality, limits opportunities, and undermines the well-being of those affected. In this chapter of *The Bounce Back Workbook*, we'll address the different dimensions of discrimination and guide you through practical steps to combat discrimination, advocate for change, and create a more inclusive environment. Despite how insidious discrimination is, it's still within our power to create a more inclusive and equitable society. By taking proactive steps, amplifying marginalized voices, and standing up against discrimination, we can build a future that celebrates diversity and embraces the inherent worth and dignity of every individual.

Reflecting on Personal Experiences

Take some time to reflect on any personal experiences of discrimination that you or someone you know may have encountered. Consider the different forms of discrimination mentioned in the main *Bounce Back* book (gender, employment, racial, age, LGBTQ+, disability) and think about how they may have impacted your life or the lives of others.

Have you ever experienced or witnessed discrimination based on gender,
   race, age, or any other characteristic? Describe what happened, and
   how it affected you or the person involved.

_____

_____

_____

_____

_____

_____.

Reflect on any other instances where you felt disadvantaged or treated
   unfairly due to discrimination. How did these situations impact your
   financial well-being or emotional state?

_____

_____

_____.

Understanding the Financial Implications
of Discrimination

Discrimination can create economic disparities and hinder financial success for individuals and communities. From the male-female gender pay
gap and the Black-white wealth gap, to housing discrimination against
LGBTQ + couples, and employment discrimination against older adults,
discrimination takes a huge financial toll.

The gender pay gap, for instance, not only affects women's current earnings but also impacts their lifetime income, savings, and retirement prospects. Similarly, the Black-white wealth gap reflects systemic disparities in
access to quality education, employment opportunities, homeownership,
and generational wealth accumulation. This wealth gap perpetuates financial inequality and limits economic mobility for Black individuals and communities. Discrimination against LGBTQ + couples in housing can lead
to limited housing choices, higher costs, and increased housing instability.
Additionally, employment discrimination against older adults can result
in reduced job prospects, lower wages, and diminished retirement savings.

These financial implications of discrimination compound over time, making it challenging for affected individuals and communities to build wealth, access affordable housing, and secure their economic well-being. Addressing and dismantling discriminatory practices is crucial for fostering an inclusive and equitable society, where everyone has equal opportunities to thrive financially and achieve their goals. It requires proactive measures such as enforcing anti-discrimination laws, promoting diversity and inclusion in all sectors, and creating equitable policies that level the playing field for historically marginalized groups. By recognizing the financial implications of discrimination, we can work toward creating a more just and equitable future for all.

Activity: Promoting Awareness and Empathy

Make a concerted effort to engage in activities that foster empathy and promote awareness of discrimination issues. This can include reading books, watching documentaries or films, attending workshops, or participating in discussions that focus on diversity, inclusion, and combating discrimination. Make a personal commitment to combating discrimination below.

To combat or increase my understanding of discrimination, I will do the following:

Step 1: _____

Step 2: _____

Step 3: _____

Reflection questions:

After you do something (such as reading a book, article, or documentary that explores the experiences of individuals facing discrimination, or maybe attending a training session focused on diversity and inclusion), write about your experience(s) below. How did your activities foster empathy within you or deepen your understanding of the challenges faced by marginalized groups?

_____

_____

_____.

Reminder: One simple strategy is to just engage in conversations with people from different backgrounds and listen to their stories. These interactions can broaden your perspective and bolster your understanding too.

Strategies for Dealing with Discrimination

Bounce Back highlighted five strategies for dealing with discrimination. These strategies include: speaking up, finding support, taking care of your mental health, educating yourself and others, and engaging in activism.

Which strategy resonates with you the most? How can you incorporate them into your personal or professional life?

_____

_____

_____.

Have you ever used any of the five strategies, such as speaking up or engaging in advocacy to oppose discrimination? If so, what happened and what caused you to act? If you have never proactively opposed discrimination, why not?

_____

_____

_____.

Brainstorm additional ways to support individuals facing discrimination. How can you advocate for equal treatment, challenge discriminatory practices, or create inclusive spaces?

_____

_____

_____.

Consider how you can contribute to organizations or initiatives that address discrimination. How can you use your skills, resources, connections, or platform to make a difference?

_____

_____

_____.

Think about the role education plays in combating discrimination. How can you educate yourself and others about the importance of equality, diversity, and inclusion?

_____

_____

_____.

What Does Workplace Discrimination Look Like?

Discrimination in the workplace doesn't just mean not getting hired because of your race or being paid less because you're a woman. There are numerous forms of workplace discrimination that you should be aware of because they can affect you or someone you care about financially. Even if you personally aren't affected, you should nonetheless want all people to be treated in a fair and just manner. But when workplace discrimination occurs, it's anything but fair. It may be overt, or hidden; it could be blatantly offensive, or take the form of subtle, passive-aggressive microaggressions. Take a look at what discrimination on the job can look like—and imagine this was you, in real life.

Employment discrimination: Imagine you're as qualified as anyone else for a job, but you're turned down because of your race or the color of your skin. This is a reality for many Black and Brown people.

Name bias: Picture yourself applying for a job, but your application is overlooked simply because your name sounds ethnic or different. Studies have shown this to be a common challenge for many people with ethnic-sounding names.

Hair discrimination: Now imagine you've styled your hair in a way that expresses your cultural identity, such as wearing an Afro, braids, twists, or dreadlocks. But at work, you're told that your natural hair is "unprofessional." This is hair discrimination, and it became so prevalent in America that a law called the CROWN Act was passed to ban race-based hair discrimination. CROWN stands for Creating a Respectful and Open World for Natural Hair.

Disability discrimination: Picture yourself as a person with a disability. You're capable and qualified, but employers doubt your abilities or aren't willing to make reasonable accommodations. This is disability discrimination, and it's like being an excellent swimmer but not being allowed to compete because the pool doesn't have an accessible entrance.

Gender discrimination: Imagine you're a woman in a male-dominated field. Despite your qualifications, you're passed over for promotions or given less-challenging assignments. This is gender discrimination, and it affects women at all levels in the work world.

Age discrimination: Now picture yourself as an older worker. You have years of experience and wisdom, but employers only want to hire younger employees, thinking they're more up-to-date or will work for less pay. This is age discrimination, and it unfairly impacts more seasoned workers.

When all these forms of discriminatory workplace practices persist, it leads to retirement inequality too. Picture a race where some runners are given a head start while others are held back. Discriminatory practices in the work environment—such as unequal pay based on gender, race, or age, limited access to retirement benefits, and disparities in promotions and career advancement opportunities—mean disenfranchised groups don't have the ability to work and earn at their full potential. They wind up later in life with less money all around.

For instance, women get to retirement with 30% less money than men and lose out an estimated $1.6 million due to the wage gap, according to data from TIAA. Additionally, TIAA reports that 54% of African Americans don't have enough money for a secure retirement. By eliminating unfair discriminatory practices in the workforce, we can start to close some of these retirement gaps too.

From an employer standpoint, workplace discrimination is also costly. In 2023, for instance, the investment firm Goldman Sachs settled a gender discrimination lawsuit and agreed to pay $215 million to former and current employees who alleged the Wall Street firm had systemically underpaid women. The settlement involved 2,800 associates and vice presidents who worked mostly in the company's investment banking, investment management, and securities division from July 2002 to March 2023. Goldman must also now engage an independent expert to review performance evaluations and pay practices to check for gender pay gaps. Plus, the bank undoubtedly racked up a ton of legal bills, since this lawsuit began in 2010.

In this case, we don't know the ages of all the women involved, of course. But it's worth noting that researchers from the National Bureau of Economic Research have found that age bias disproportionately impacts older female workers, particularly those near retirement age. That's a double whammy against you if you're an older woman in the workplace, and a triple whammy if you're an older Black woman. Unfortunately, lots of discrimination is intersectional in nature.

What Does Housing Discrimination Look Like?

Have you or someone you know ever experienced housing discrimination or witnessed its effects? From redlining and exclusionary zoning rules to predatory mortgage lending and appraisal bias, housing-related discrimination perpetuates major inequalities and disparities in US society. These practices have had a significant financial impact on individuals and communities, perpetuating economic disparities and hindering wealth accumulation. Here's what housing discrimination looks like. Picture yourself navigating these circumstances.

Redlining: Imagine looking at a map of your city and seeing certain neighborhoods marked in red, signaling them as "risky" or "undesirable." This was the practice of redlining, where banks and financial institutions would refuse loans or services to people living in these areas, often predominantly Black neighborhoods. This historic practice has left a lasting legacy of economic disparity that many Black families still experience today.

Appraisal gap: Now picture yourself as a homeowner, proud of your property, and ready to sell or refinance. However, when the appraiser arrives, they undervalue your home compared to similar homes in predominantly white neighborhoods. This is the appraisal gap, and it disproportionately affects many Black homeowners.

Predatory lending: Now let's say you have great credit and you've even managed to save up for a house, a piece of the American Dream. But when you go to the bank to get a mortgage, you're steered into higher-cost "subprime" loans, or the terms are much harsher, simply because of your race. This is predatory lending, often targeted toward people of color and low-income individuals.

Racial steering: Picture a real estate agent showing you homes only in certain neighborhoods, steering you away from others based on your race or ethnicity. This is racial steering, and it limits choices and perpetuates residential segregation.

Exclusionary zoning: Now imagine you're looking for affordable housing, but local zoning laws limit the construction of multifamily or low-income housing units in certain areas. This is exclusionary zoning, which often disproportionately affects people of color and low-income families.

Disability discrimination: Picture yourself as a person with a disability. You might find that many homes aren't accessible to you or landlords refuse to make reasonable accommodations. This is a form of disability discrimination in housing. It limits your housing choices and can lead to increased financial burdens as you seek accessible housing.

Taken as a whole, discriminatory housing practices have had profound financial implications for individuals and communities. They have limited opportunities for wealth accumulation, hindered homeownership rates, and perpetuated racial and economic disparities. Denied access to fair mortgage terms, affordable housing options, and equal opportunities in homeownership, individuals and communities face barriers to building equity and financial stability.

Examining Structural Inequality and Discrimination in Your Environment

Think about the systems that you interact with daily or regularly (e.g. the banking system, your workplace, the government, the health care system). Write down how each of these systems either helps or hinders your financial health and the financial health of others. What type of discrimination do you think occurs within these each of these systems?

Banking system: _____

_____

_____.

The workplace: _____

_____

_____.

The government: _____

_____

_____.

Health care system: _____

_____

_____.

Educational system: _____

_____

_____.

Once you consider how structural issues, such as racism or discrimination, may have impacted your financial standing and others' too, reflecting on these systems may reveal opportunities for advocacy, change, or different choices.

To play your part in helping to reduce discrimination, you can also take a number of proactive steps and engage in various activities to fight discrimination or raise awareness of it and its ramifications.

Suggested Activities

✓ Organize a panel discussion or seminar featuring speakers from diverse racial backgrounds to share their experiences with discrimination and its financial consequences.

✓ Create an awareness campaign using social media platforms to highlight the financial impact of racial discrimination.

Activity: Shed Light on LGBTQ+ Discrimination

Organize an in-person event or webinar featuring LGBTQ+ individuals sharing their experiences. A few ideas:

- Explore the financial consequences of employment bias against LGBTQ+ individuals;
- Explore how limited access to health care for members of the LGBTQ+ community harms them physically, emotionally, and financially;
- Explore the impact of housing and adoption discrimination on the financial stability of LGBTQ+ individuals and families;
- Brainstorm strategies to promote LGBTQ+ rights, fight discrimination, and foster financial equality.

Reflection questions:

- How can speaking up and finding support empower any individuals who have experienced discrimination?

_____

_____.

- What are some effective ways to discuss discrimination in the workplace?

_____

_____.

- How does engaging in activism help people regain control and fight against discrimination, while also preventing future instances of harm?

_____

_____.

Create a vision board or visual representation of your financial and personal aspirations, incorporating the principles of resilience and inclusivity. What will be on your board and why?

_____

_____

_____

_____.

Reflect on the importance of resilience and a positive mindset in overcoming financial challenges and discrimination. Consider the all-around social and financial advantages of combating injustices and promoting inclusivity.

How can the lessons learned about discrimination contribute to your individual long-term economic well-being and emotional wellness?

_____

_____

_____

_____.

As we conclude this twelfth chapter of _The Bounce Back Workbook_, which focused on discrimination, take time to think about what you have just done, felt, and discovered. What emotions surfaced for you during the exercises? What lessons have you learned so far, and what growth have you experienced? Write a recap below.

_____

_____

_____

_____

Tying It All Together

I'm so grateful to have been with you on this journey of personal discovery, emotional healing, and financial improvement. Thank you for trusting me to partner with you and for getting this far. I congratulate you on your willingness to learn, as well as your perseverance and grit. I would also love to hear from you—everything from your struggles to your successes. So feel free to email me directly at info@AskTheMoneyCoach.com and put "Bounce Back reader" in the subject line to help me prioritize inbox messages and my responses. I'd be especially honored if you shared with me any progress you've made in recovering from any of the Dreaded Ds.

For now, please write a personal reflection on the insights you have gained from completing *The Bounce Back Workbook* and how you plan to apply various lessons to your own life.

_____

_____

_____

_____.

How have you grown in resilience or mindset while completing *The Bounce Back Workbook?*

_____

_____

_____

_____.

Remember to take the time to reflect on your personal experiences, engage in the suggested activities, and answer the prompts and reflection questions honestly and thoughtfully. By doing so, you can sharpen yourself, your strengths, and your capacity to grow despite any situation.

Final Activity: Writing Your New Bounce Back Story

Do you remember in Chapter 1 of this *Workbook* that I had you write your own comeback story? Now that you've made it this far, I want you to revisit this concept. Imagine yourself successfully overcoming any Dreaded Ds you currently face. Write a detailed narrative of your journey, highlighting the key actions you took, the main lessons you learned, and the personal growth you experienced. Remember the Transition Truths: You have a say – and can therefore write your own narrative. Every transition is a new beginning. What do you want yours to be?

_____

_____

_____

_____

_____.

Use this final activity—and all the exercises in *The Bounce Back Workbook*—as customized tools and reminders of your uniqueness and strength. The *Workbook* exercises can reinforce your belief in your ability to handle change, transition safely, and overcome obstacles. In the future, as you learn more and gain new insights, please revisit the contents of this *Workbook* and revise or update your story regularly. Feel free to also explore topics anew, reflect further with a fresh perspective, and add new discoveries, epiphanies, or aha moments you've experienced during your resilience-building journey. If you stumble or encounter future setbacks, you can now face those situations with greater ease, knowing you are equipped to *bounce back stronger than ever!*

Research Resources

Introduction

N/A

Chapter 1: Resilience and Grit

N/A

Chapter 2: Building Your Resilience

Budget Worksheet from the author – uploaded into portal
Net Worth Worksheet from the author – uploaded into portal

Chapter 3: Downsized from a Job

N/A

Chapter 4: Divorce

N/A

Chapter 5: Death of a Loved One

N/A

Chapter 6: Disability

SSDI 2023 maximum payment level and average amount
https://evansdisability.com/blog/social-security-disability-benefits-pay-chart/

SSDI general info via Fact Sheet from SSA
https://www.ssa.gov/pubs/EN-05-11001.pdf

Chapter 7: Disease

Info about RIP Medical Debt
https://ripmedicaldebt.org/

Cleveland, Toledo, and Cook County cancel medical debt
https://nextcity.org/urbanist-news/rip-medical-debt-toledo-chicago-cancel-hospital-bills

Mackenzie Scott's $80 million in donations to RIP Medical Debt
https://www.ripmedicaldebt.org/press-release/mackenzie-scott-makes-impactful-30-million-gift-to-rip-medical-debt-for-a-second-time/

Texas church buys and forgives medical debt
https://covenant.org/covenant-donation-abolishes-more-than-16m-in-area-medical-debt/

Crossroads church buys and abolishes medical debt
https://www.cincinnati.com/story/news/2020/02/24/crossroads-church-nonprofit-wipe-out-46-5-million-medical-debt/4854753002/

Trinity Moravian Church buys and cancels medical debt
https://independenttribune.com/news/state-and-regional/3-million-
medical-debt-forgiven-trinity-moravian-winston-salem-davie-
yadkin-davidson/article_4c3d9a35-8029-5f76-932f-09a63ec7843b.html

Chapter 8: Disasters

State Farm and Allstate stopped selling insurance in California
https://www.latimes.com/business/story/2023-06-02/allstate-state-
farm-stop-selling-new-home-insurance-in-california

Chapter 9: Debt

Edmunds online tool to calculate the true cost of car ownership, including depreciation
https://www.edmunds.com/tco.html

AAA's Your Driving Cost study on the annual cost of new car ownership
https://newsroom.aaa.com/2022/08/annual-cost-of-new-car-
ownership-crosses-10k-mark/

AAA Online Driving Costs Calculator
https://www.aaa.com/autorepair/drivingcosts

Biden Administration announces efforts to offer student loan relief
https://www.whitehouse.gov/briefing-room/statements-
releases/2023/06/30/fact-sheet-president-biden-announces-
new-actions-to-provide-debt-relief-and-support-for-student-
loan-borrowers/

Chapter 10: Damaged Credit

Factors in FICO Credit Score calculation
https://www.myfico.com/credit-education/whats-in-your-credit-score

Center for LGBTQ Economic Advancement & Research Survey on LGBTQ credit scores
https://lgbtq-economics.org/wp-content/uploads/2021/06/The-
Economic-Well-Being-of-LGBT-Adults-in-2019.pdf

Chapter 11: Dollar Deficits

N/A

Chapter 12: Discrimination

CROWN Act
https://www.thecrownact.com/about

TIAA retirement inequality data on women and African Americans
https://retireinequality.com/

Goldman Sachs settles gender discrimination lawsuit for $215 million
https://apnews.com/article/goldman-sachs-settlement-gender-equity-b9373d369cb70165565ec83abe03b8c3

National Bureau of Economic Research study on age discrimination in the workplace
https://www.nber.org/papers/w21669

Appendix A
Budget Worksheet

Date: _____ Name(s):_____

Net Income	
Description	**Amount**
Salary/Wages	
Overtime	
Bonuses	
Commissions or Tips	
Part-Time Work or Second Job	
Self-Employment or Freelance Income	
Dividends, Rental, or Investment Income	
Other (Soc. Sec., Pension, TANF, SNAP)	
Total Income	$

Total Monthly Income	$

Instructions: Fill in worksheet with monthly amounts. Be honest! Enter a 0 or leave blank any line where no income or bill exists. For income earned or expenses incurred annually or irregulary, add up or estimate the total over a year, and then divide the total figure by 12 in order to calculate the average monthly amount.

Goals: This detailed Budget Worksheet will give you greater clarity about your true monthly spending.

You want to generate positive cash flow and have a properly aligned budget in which your monthly net income/take-home pay exceeds your expenses. Ideally, you will have a budget surplus, not a deficit.

Housing Expenses		Consumer Debts	
Description	**Payment**	**Description**	**Payment**
Home Mortgage or Rent		Credit Card Bill #1	
Home Equity Loan or Line of Credit		Credit Card Bill #2	
Property Taxes		Credit Card Bill #3	
Mortgage/Costs for Vacation/Rental Home		Credit Card Bill #4	
Owners Assn./Condo Fees, Repairs/Other		All Other Credit Card Bills	
Total Housing Expenses	$	Student Loans	
		Back Taxes	
Insurance Expenses		Medical Debts	
Description	**Payment**	Personal/ Unsecured/ Payday Loans	
Homeowners or Renters Insurance		Life Insurance/ Investment Loans	
Earthquake or Flood Insurance		Auto Loans or Car Leases	
Health Insurance		Other Debts Owed	
Life Insurance		**Total Consumer Debts**	$
Disability Insurance			
Car Insurance		**Utilities/ Services**	
Umbrella Liability Insurance		**Description**	**Payment**
Long-Term Care Insurance		Gas/Heating Bill	
Other Insurance		Electricity/Light Bill	
Total Insurance Expenses	$	Water Bill	
		Cell Phone #1	

Personal Expenses		Cell Phone #2	
Description	**Payment**	Landline Phone	
Savings (Rainy Day/ Emergency Fund, etc.)		Trash Bill	
Food/Groceries and Household Supplies		Garden, Lawn, or Pool Care	
Eating Out (Restaurants, Fast Food, Bars)		Internet/Cable/ Satellite TV	
Entertainment or Hobbies		CPA/Tax/ Financial/Legal/ Mental	
Clothes/Shopping/ Discretionary Spending		Maid or House- keeping	
Gas for Car, Repairs/ Transportation Costs		Other Utilities	
Memberships or Subscriptions		Other Services	
Personal Care (hair, nails, gym, spa, etc.)		**Total Utility/ Service Expenses**	$
Travel/Vacations (air, hotel, rental car, etc.)			
Pets (pet food/toys, vet bills, kennel fees)		**Gifts/Presents/ Donations**	
Other Miscellaneous/ Personal Expenses		**Description**	**Amount**
Total Personal Expenses	$	Anniversary or Wedding Gifts	
		Birthday Gifts or Graduation Gifts	
Expenses for Kids/Adult Children		Valentine's Day	
Description	**Payment**	Mother's Day	
School or College Tuition and Fees		Father's Day	
Room and Board		4th of July	
Summer Programs (Camp/Pre-College etc.)		Labor Day or Halloween	
Extra-Curricular Activities		Thanksgiving	

Sports (uniforms /program fees, clinics, etc.)		Christmas, Hanukkah, or Kwanzaa	
Lessons/Tutors (academic/ artistic/music)		New Year's Eve	
Child's Car (payments, insurance, gas, etc.)		Tithes, Offerings, Donations	
Day Care/Babysitter/Nanny		Cash/Loans to Family/Friends	
Allowance/Other Expenses for Children		Other Holidays/ Gifts/Presents	
Total Expenses for Kids/Adult Children	$	**Total Gifts/ Presents/ Donations**	$

Total Monthly Expenses	$	**Monthly Income – Expenses**	$

Monthly Budget surplus or deficit?	

Budget Worksheet Copyright: Lynnette Khalfani-Cox, The Money Coach®

Appendix B

Net Worth Statement

Date: _____ Name(s): _____

Cash/Liquid Assets	
Description	**Amount**
Checking Accounts	
Savings Accounts	
Money Market Accounts	
Cash Value of Permanent Life Insurance	
Other Cash on Hand	
Total Cash/Liquid Assets	**$**

Investment Assets	
Description	**Amount**
401(k) Retirement Plan	
403(b), 457, or Thrift Savings Plan	
Pension Assets	
IRAs (Traditional, Roth, or *my*RA)	

Instructions: Fill in statement with total amounts using actual values or estimates as necessary for the market value of assets such as homes, cars, furniture, jewelry, and art work. Enter a 0 on any line where no asset or liability exists.

Goals: Your net worth shows you a snapshot of your current financial standing. You calculate your net worth by adding up all your assets (what you own) and then subtracting all your liabilities (what you owe). You want your net worth to be positive and growing over time.

To give yourself an annual financial checkup, and to assess your economic progress, you should review your net worth at least once a year. Ideally, you should check your net worth quarterly or even monthly.

SEP or SIMPLE Plans	
Stocks	
Bonds	
Mutual Funds	
529 Plans	
Annuities or Trust Assets	
Other Investments	
Total Investment Assets	$

Liabilities	
Description	**Amount**
Mortgage Balance: Primary Home	
Home Equity Loan/ Line of Credit	
2nd Home/Rental/ Vacation Debts	
Auto Loans or Lease Balances	
Credit Card Debts	
Student Loans	
Back Taxes	
401(k) or Retirement Plan Loans	
Personal/Unsecured/ Payday Loans	
Life Insurance Loans	
Other Debts Owed	
Total Liabilities	$

Property/Non-Liquid Assets	
Description	**Amount**
Market Value of Home/ Primary Residence	
2nd Home/Vacation Property/Timeshare	
Value of Rental/Investment Property	
Market Value of Cars (use KBB.com 4 est)	
Household Items (furniture/electronics etc.)	
Personal Items (furs/ clothing/jewelry etc.)	
Art, Collectibles, and Other Property	
Total Property/ Non-Liquid Assets	$

Total Assets	$

Assets − Liabilities = Net Worth	$
Net Worth: Positive or Negative?	

Net Worth Statement Copyright: Lynnette Khalfani-Cox, The Money Coach and Co-Founder of http://AskTheMoneyCoach.com

Index